SAI

The Age of Cosmic Family

Published by
Lotus Press

SAI
The Age of Cosmic Family

Sudarshan

Lotus Press
4263/3, Ansari Road,
Darya Ganj, New Delhi-110002

Lotus Press
4263/3, Ansari Road, Darya Ganj, New Delhi- 110002
Ph.: 32903912, 23280047, E-mail: lotus_press@sify.com
www.lotuspress.co.in

SAI *The Age of Cosmic Family*

ISBN: 81-901912-5-X
Reprint: 2007

Published by: Lotus Press, New Delhi.
Laser Typeset by: Aruna Enterprises, Delhi-110 094.
Printed at: Gyan Sagar, Delhi.

Contents

1.	Introduction	1
2.	Sai: The Earthly Form	4-10
3.	The Greatness of Sai	11-25
4.	Sai's *Leelas*	26-82
5.	Sai's Bestowal of Grace	83-137
6.	Sai's Clairvoyance	138-147
7.	Sustainable Directions	148-157
8.	Preachings of Mortality	158-163
9.	Creator's Creation	164-167

1

Introduction

Sai is the divine boat who ferries his disciples as travellers across the ocean of life to the shore of bliss. He is the Ultimate Truth pervading in every being, who is a sea of kindness, the highest bliss and who is the ultimate destination. He is the compassionate one, the cosmic consciousness in all beings, the seat of Supreme Knowledge, who, as the sustainer of the universe, pervades it.

There is no doubt that Sai is the Supreme Spirit and Divine Energy who descended on earth with a mission to perform, the wonders of which are etched in all hearts for posterity. He is the sustainer of the universe, and a personification of the highest renunciation.

During his early years, his activities were centred around those who were with him, and focused on social obligations. The people benefited largely, and this led to the development and spread of Sai faith in a big way all over the world. The main benefit though was the unification of *dharma* and religion, of the Hindu faith and the Islam faith within themselves, and of the purification and refinement of both, thus building up a common flame of unity. And Sai showed himself as all pervading, as *Atman* or Soul of all.

Sai stressed upon the importance of birth as a human being. It was not merely living a mundane existence that distinguished a human from other beings, for did not animals and plants also live and breathe? Man was designed for higher purposes, and for him to evolve to higher and higher planes till he reached the ultimate goal, he had to realise his Self and become one with It. Being emancipated, he had to be fearless, free and everlasting. To have this awareness itself was the fulfilment of this birth.

Sai also emphasised the importance of devotion to and faith in one's *guru*. Single-minded meditation on the *guru* transformed one into speechless silence, leaving nothing separate from him, but being merged into him. By virtue of his loving devotion, a devotee would never brag about his knowledge, but offer his body, mind and wealth at his *guru's* feet, i.e., surrender his all to him.

Endowed with divine powers, Sai could leave his body at will and return to it at the appropriate time. He could weave out miraculous deeds, not with any intention of showing his prowess, but to inculcate faith in his disciples, so that they could awake from ignorance and realise their Self. He averted accidents, cured diseases, predicted happenings of the future, bestowed grace on whoever came to him for his *darshan*, explained passages from the *Gita* which he had never read, and took part in all celebrations, irrespective of class and creed.

Baba took human form to do good to others, and when his mission was achieved, merged in the end, into the unmanifest.

2

Sai: The Earthly Form

Sai (Infinity) took to human form in this world with a definite purpose, a mission to fulfil, so that his love and light may be assimilated by all. In his quiet, unassuming way, he taught the principles of "Universe as one cosmic family", prescribing, both by example and precept, valuable remedies for spiritual unification. He gave his devotees a common bond of love for him, after having shown them the essence of spirituality. His life and teachings embodied the most forceful exposition of the underlying unity of all communities and creeds of the world.

People often fail to attain the highest goal of human existence since they fail to observe *dharma,* and hence *Infinity* took to human form to re-establish *dharma.* In various corners of the earth, people had started indulging in vices, totally neglecting opportunities for self-upliftment, ignoring their health hazards and early symptoms of ill-health, and turning away from the spiritual path by centring their interest in wealth, family and prosperity. Infinity (Sai) then took form to emancipate such souls, to uplift the low and poorly, and to lay a solid foundation around the crumbling structure of worldly life, so that the devotees were redeemed of their noxious ways.

Baba's simple, yet spiritually evolved way of life, with its supreme detachment and renunciation, and his style of functioning, imparting spiritual instruction and guidance to the devotees through experiences and instances in their daily life, have a lasting appeal. Revealing himself age after age, as he claims, for protecting the good and destroying the evil, he established, once again, righteousness in the world.

As the universal guru, he used the divine powers with which he was blessed, to help and protect the good, taking them on the right path of spirituality and higher evolvement. His devotees absorbed more and more of his nature by constantly residing in their hearts, so that they grew more into life, light and love. This evolvement was quite infectious, affecting the lives of those around them in such a way as to bring out the goodness in others. All, who came in contact with them grew into morally and spiritually better beings. He was like a magnet drawing his devotees to him forcefully, rubbing off his influence and divine love on to them.

EARLY YEARS

Baba first manifested Himself for the sake of His Bhaktas, under the *neem* (margosa) tree as a young lad of about sixteen. The villagers were amazed to see His divine form and the hard penance that He did. He did not go to anybody's house and was oblivious of heat and rain and was in divine bliss. Under a flat stone were found four burning lamps and a corridor leading to a cellar where 'cow-mouth' shaped structures, wooden boards and necklaces were seen. Khandoba said this lad practised penance for 12 years here. The people began to question the lad about this. He diverted the question by telling them that this was His Guru's place and requested them to guard it well.

The young fakir had for a time, disappeared from Shirdi, but later with the marriage party of a Muslim gentleman named Chand Patil, he once again came to Shirdi. Let us listen to that story.

Chand Patil lived in Dhoopkheda, a village of Aurangabad district. Once while travelling towards Aurangabad, he lost his mare, which for two months could not be traced. Patil was very fond of his mare and felt sorry and distressed over this loss. Finally he flung the saddle across his back and set off for home.

Leaving Aurangabad behind, he travelled about nine miles. There was a mango tree on the way, under which he saw a *fakir* with a cap in his hand, body covered by a *kafni* (mendicant's robe), and a baton under the armpit. As he crushed some tobacco in the palm of his hand and filled the *chillum* (clay pipe), a wonderful thing happened.

As Chand Patil was passing by, the *fakir* called out to him by name. Chandbhai was surprised that a stranger should know his name. Baba asked him to rest with him for a while, and asked about the saddle in his hand. Chand Patil stated that he had lost his mare. Baba told him to search for his mare 'Bijli' along the rivulet that ran close by. Chand Patil was astonished to find his mare so quickly, but what amazed him more than anything else was that a total stranger should know his name as well as that of his mare, besides her location. He thought that he must have met a sage who had no limit to his miracles, and who was no ordinary human being. He brought his mare and sat beside the *fakir*.

Baba picked up a pair of tongs, thrust it in the soil, and brought out a burning coal from it. This he placed in the *chillum* (pipe) in his hand. He then took up his *sataka* (baton) with his other hand, and struck the ground hard with it. Water immediately welled out. He dipped a strip of cloth in it and then wound it round his *chillum*. He then picked up the *chillum* and started smoking; he then asked Patil to do the same. Chand Patil was quite dazed by all that he had witnessed.

Patil then pressed the *fakir* by paying him a visit. The *fakir*, who had come to this earth only for such divine *leela*, conferred the favour on him. The next day he went to the village to stay with the Patil, and spent about three years there.

Chand Patil was the headman of the village Dhoopkheda and his wife's nephew was engaged to be married to a girl from Shirdi. So, with the bullock-carts and horses, the marriage party set out for Shirdi, in due course. And then, Baba, drawn by his affection for Chandbhai, joined the party, too!

The marriage party, as it arrived, stopped under the banyan tree near the Khandoba temple. The bullocks were all unyoked in the yard, in the Khandoba temple compound. And Baba, too, got down there along with all the others. As this youthful *fakir* alighted from the cart, it was Bhagat Mahlsapati, the *pujari* of Khandoba temple, who first saw him and received him with the words "Welcome Sai". From then onwards, that name became his popular name. Thereafter, people began to call him 'Sai' and the name came to be used commonly by all.

Baba's old devotees recognised him and requested him not to go away from Shirdi. Thus, Sai Baba, who first came as a *fakir* to Shirdi, left it for three years and returned with Chand Patil's marriage party, made Shirdi his permanent abode. There was no place he could call his own, for though everything was his, nothing was his. He had no attachment to any place or person; though countless in Shirdi had relationships with him through previous births.

So Baba took shelter under a margosa tree, close to his Guru's tomb. But as it did not provide enough shelter, he chose a dilapidated mosque for residing in.

Here he lit the lamps filled with water instead of oil since it was denied to him by some oil vendors who were out to watch him squirm. But to their sheer amazement they saw the lamps burning brightly and quickly realised the greatness of the *fakir*. Here was a man who could produce whatever he wanted by mere will power or supreme command.

The old dilapidated mosque, where Sai spent almost 65 years is called *Dwarkamai*. The mosque was the place where people thronged to offer oblations to Baba, worshipping his feet, where *bhajans* were sung and *Aarti* offered, and where food was distributed to the people.

Baba shared his food with all the beings of his surroundings, be they human or animal. His doctrine was simple — all were beings created by the Almighty, and all were equal in His eyes.

In his early years, Baba used to cure people with various kinds of herbs, but later he blessed all people with *udhi* (sacred ashes). His miracles were of curing varied illnesses, removing poverty, curing barrenness in women, warding off diseases and epidemics, lighting lamps with water, forecasting calamities, controlling the elements like fire and storms, etc. By such innumerable miracles, he not only cured, helped and comforted all his devotees and visitors, but also taught them the most subtle spiritual truths.

Baba lived amidst common folk as a penniless *fakir*, wearing a torn *kafni*, sleeping on a mat, resting his head on a brick that was his lifelong companion, and begging for alms. In his lifetime he had no possessions, did not accept any specific school of thought or discipline, and laid no importance on caste, creed, doctrines, dogmas or status. But in spite of all this, he is revered by Hindus, Muslims, Buddhists, Parsis and Christians alike.

Baba had disciples from all religions, and taught them the same values that set him apart as a greatly revered man. To the Hindus, he was the *Poorna-avatar* (the Perfect Incarnation of God), well-versed in Hindu scriptures. To the Muslims, he was a *fakir* living in a mosque, observing the disciplines of Islam, who used to utter, "Allah Malik hai!" To the Parsis, he was the sacred fire-worshipper. His philosophy included the essence of Christ's sermon and the eight-fold path of the Buddha. Sai allowed his devotees to follow their own traditional beliefs and religious modes of worship and taught "let the different faiths exist, let them flourish and let the glory of the Infinity be sung in all languages and in a variety of tunes. Respect the differences between the faiths and recognise them as valid as long as they do not extinguish the flame of Unity". The unified flame of love and faith should bring 'Integral Perfection', where we should see the 'Cosmic Family'.

3

The Greatness of Sai

Sai Baba led the life of a simple *fakir*, dressed in torn clothes, and lived on alms at Shirdi; he showed by example that all living creatures have the same soul, and hence should be loved, cared for and helped by all. His divine assurance to his devotees that merely by remembering him at the hour of need, he would help them, is a source of eternal inspiration to the Cosmic Family.

Sai Baba not only guides, helps and liberates devotees who earnestly pray to him, but he blesses them with his divine grace. Being very human, he showed his sympathy and compassion for living beings. He was the embodiment of dispassion and was an enigma to all. People soon discovered by their experiences of his divine miracles and compassionate help that he was beyond an ordinary saint, a divine personality of a very high order. Uttering the name of 'Allah' most of the time, he always advocated the worship and veneration of God, by whatever name they called Him.

Baba disliked the practice of untouchability, dowry, religious conversions and fundamentalism, casteism, and the traditional barring of women in certain matters of worship and social life. He announced that all gods and goddesses were within him, for he was Krishna, he was Shiva, he was Dattatreya, he is the Divine Being then, now and forever. An instance in point follows.

Balwant C. Kohojkar, a retired officer, came to Shirdi in 1911, when Datta Jayanti was celebrated. Around 5 p.m., while all sat around Baba in the mosque, Baba suddenly cried out, "I am having the pangs of labour! I cannot bear it! I am about to deliver." Soon, he asked everyone to vacate the mosque, and after some time, he summoned them in. He seemed immensely pleased, and when Balwant trooped in with others, he was astonished to see the three-faced figure of Datta in Baba's seat. In a trice, this image disappeared, and Baba appeared seated in his place.

Today, Shirdi Sai Baba's name has spread worldwide, and Sai shelters are devoted to him throughout India, and in foreign countries like the United States, Canada, Britain, South Africa, Australia, etc. Devotional songs are sung here to invoke his grace.

Baba's uniqueness or greatness cannot be questioned or in doubt. He said about himself thus:

> "I am not confined within this body of three and a half cubits height; I am everywhere; see

me in every place."

"I am the Inner Ruler of all hearts and seated in their hearts."

"I am the Controller — the wirepuller of the show of this Universe."

"I am omnipresent, occupying land, air, country, world, light and heaven, and I am not limited."

"I am the Mother—origin of all senses, the Creator, Preserver and Destroyer. Nothing will harm him who turns his attention towards Me, but *Maya* will lash or whip him who forgets Me. All the insects, ants, the visible, movable and immovable world are in My Body or Form."

"People think they are all different from each other. But in this, they are wrong. I am inside you. You are inside Me."

These statements put to rest any doubts about his being Supreme. He demonstrated this several times in various ways, and only those who experienced his divinity are blessed, for they are pure and have absolute faith in him. They are the ones who lived with him, and became his true devotees. By asserting 'Allah Malik hai' he implied that He is the Infinity.

Sai Baba spoke freely and mixed with all people and creatures, took part in singing and dancing, shared his food that he had collected by begging from houses with everyone. Yet he was always mentally balanced, aware of all that was going on around him, and while the world slept, he was ever awake. He saw divinity in all things, and hence treated all beings as equal.

Once Bapu Saheb Jog asked Sai Baba, "I have served you faithfully all these years, with great devotion. How will I know when its fruits come?"

Baba replied, "That fruition will bring joy to both of us, but that will be when you don a *kafni* and beg for your food like I do."

The significance of this statement was that Bapu Saheb Jog should free himself from all worldly and sensory attachments, and identify himself with God.

Baba, who had realised his identity with the Imperishable, said, "I got embodied by *Karma*, and came to a body. So I got a name and abode. *Dehi*, that is, the embodied, is my name; and the world is my abode. Infinity is my father and Maya, mother. I am the Attributeless, Absolute, Nirguna. I have no name and no residence."

Mrs. Tarabai Sadashiv Tarkhad stated of Baba, "One's first impression of Baba was derived from his eyes. There was such power and penetration in his glance that none could continue to look at his eyes. One felt that Sai Baba was reading him or her through and through. Soon one lowered one's eyes and bowed down."

Sai Baba was satiated in all his desires, fulfilled, content with what was ordained, constantly self-absorbed, and beyond joys and sorrows. As Mrs. Tarkhad says, "Not only was he present at all places when his physical body was in one place, say the mosque, but he was also able to do various things with his invisible body."

Sai Baba was, and is, always there, to place his hand of benediction on one's head as one would place it on his feet in total surrender. To quote Mrs. Tarkhad again, "One felt that he was not only in one's heart but in every atom of one's body. A few words, a gesture would reveal to one that Sai Baba knew all about the past, present and even future and about everything else. There was nothing else to do for one, except to submit trustfully and to surrender oneself to him. And there he was to look after every minute detail, and guide one safe, through every turn and every vicissitude of life. He was the *Antaryami*, call him God or *Satpurusha* in *Sahaja Stithi* or what you like. But the overpowering personality was there, and in his presence no doubts, no fears, no questionings had any place and one resigned oneself and found that was the only course, the safest and the best course.

"His *Antaryamitva*, i.e., his being inside every creature and every object, animate or inanimate, so as to control all voluntary and involuntary movements of creatures and objects throw light on what he occasionally said of himself, 'I am not confined within the three and a half cubit length of flesh, bone and blood that people call Sai Baba. I am in every dog, cat, pig, man and woman'."

As a personification of the highest renunciation, Sai Baba is the protector of this universe. In innumerable ways Baba tried to bring to the devotees a comprehension of the Formless One. According to the level that one had reached spiritually, he would treat them likewise. For instance, he would make them sit apart, he would deny *darshan* to some for long periods, he would send one away from Shirdi for a certain period, confine another in solitude in Shirdi itself, someone else was confined to the *wada* and made to read the *Pothi* (sacred text) regularly. The reason behind these strange ways was to create in them, after pursuing such a deep study over the years, a great longing for Baba's presence in an unmanifest form, always feeling his presence while eating, sitting or sleeping.

Baba was always calm, remarkably unruffled, guileless, forgiving to the utmost, forbearing by nature, and self-contained. Being omniscient, and omnipresent, he could go off to space in an invisible body. Baba was living and operating in other worlds also, besides this world and in an invisible body. . . Baba was frequently talking. . . . In the morning, sitting near his *dhuni* (fire) with several devotees, he would say to what distant place he went overnight and what he had done. Those who had slept by his side the whole night at the masjid or *chavadi* knew that his physical body was at Shirdi all the night. But his statements were literally true and were occasionally verified and found to be true. He had travelled to distant places in an invisible, i.e., spirit form and rendered help there. . . . He also made occasional references to what his function was in the terrestrial sphere and in other worlds. He several times referred to his control of the destinies of departed souls—indicating thereby his function in the Cosmic Order.

Sai Baba was a unique phenomenon, and not an ordinary saint. He was gifted with the ability to be always in and outside the material world simultaneously. Always being in the all-knowing state, he had no need to be in a trance to be unaware of his body, self and surroundings to reach a higher state of knowledge. Mrs. Tarkhad says, "He was every moment exercising a double consciousness, one actively utilising the Ego called Sai Baba and dealing with other egos in temporal and spiritual affairs, and, the other entirely superseding all egos and resting in the position of the Universal Soul or Ego." He used and manifested all the powers and potentials incidental to both the states of consciousness.

Baba always said, "Allah Malik hai", and that he was a mere servant of Him, but to a devotee he appeared to be God. Baba always insisted that there could be no spiritual liberation from bondage if one did not acquire moral freedom.

Baba was himself the refuge and support for all his

devotees. He was indulgent, caring for their feelings. Though appearing to be stationed in Shirdi, he moved everywhere quite freely. Detached and unruffled as he was, he would accept from them the various rituals of *puja*, from each according to his faith. He allowed them to wash his hands and feet, apply sandal-paste on his forehead, wave the fan gently to keep away flies from him, play musical instruments, etc.

Sai Baba was quite enigmatic and people were truly aware of his divinity. The best way to understand him well was to experience him. Though he is no longer manifest in a human form, his spirit is here to guide people who seek him. This is borne out by actual observations and experiences that people have had, who say that he is more active than ever before. Justice M.B. Rege states, "I feel that he is always with me. At times, he visibly shows his form to reassure me or guide me." One need not have intelligence or capacity to experience him, only total faith, pure and unadulterated. All one need do is to take one step towards him, and he will surely take several more towards you to help you in your life's journey towards God-realisation.

Baba's human form on earth was totally devoid of blame or sin, for he was a wonderful model of ethical perfection. He showed by example that he was a great unifying and universalising force. He taught the values of brotherhood and the means to overcome petty barriers between man and man. His tolerant views, universality and non-discrimination are a unique and matchless phenomena. He taught people how to recognise the presence of the Divinity in all beings.

Baba did not expect everyone to come to him as a perfect being, for he was there in his mission to mould such beings, change their views, and educate them to understand, appreciate and worship God. He wished to convince them, if they were Hindus, that he was Vishnu, Narayana, etc., and allowed water to flow from his feet, as Ganga did from Vishnu's feet. Though they believed him to be a great being, one devotee's doubts were not wiped out totally, for though he sprinkled a few drops of the holy water coursing from Baba's feet on his head, he refused to drink it, for was he not a Muslim Vishnu? Such foolish thoughts made them blind to Sai Baba's divinity, and only a few people like S.B. Dhumal saw clearly that Baba was neither a Hindu nor a Muslim, but above all castes, sects and religions. And clearly people accepted Baba's claim that he is the *Paramaṭma* in all beings.

Being extremely proficient in concentration, Sai Baba had reached the perfection of merging the self with the Self. Advocating absolute selfless service to society, Baba, though always Self-absorbed, never failed in his social contacts with his neighbours.

He ploughed the common land, on which his *Samadhi Mandir* now stands, and turned it into a flower garden. This he himself nurtured, watering the plants, carrying pots of water on his shoulder for watering them. Never making any invidious distinction between Hindus and Muslims, he sent the flowers and leaves from his garden to temples and masjids. His attitude towards all was motherly, and he considered all castes, creeds, sects, religions as non-existent or trivial, for he was in a supreme realised state.

He always lit up three or four earthen lamps in the mosque, as was the custom common to both Hindu and Muslim faiths. Hence he went around the village begging for oil from oil vendors. There were only two shops which sold oil in Shirdi.

One day some of them decided to have fun at his expense, little realising the consequences. They refused to supply him with oil, saying that they had none. The young *fakir* returned to the mosque without uttering a word of protest.

Those who intended to watch the fun, followed him to the mosque. Baba filled the four lamps with the water from the jar that was kept there. He placed a cotton wick in each, and lighted the lamps. To everyone's amazement the lamps burned brightly. The sudden nudging and tittering gave place to great awe, and realising Baba's divinity, they fell at his feet, seeking his pardon. There was no more talk then of the *fakir* as 'crazy'. They soon found that he was a unique saint and teacher with boundless compassion for the lesser beings. These devotees, being true to their Guru, served him by carrying faggots, cooking, sweeping, lighting up the fire, washing his clothes, and other menial jobs with great joy, devotion and contentment. All this Baba accepted for he had no attachment or self-conceit, and realised himself as the pure soul that cannot be tainted by such service.

There were times Baba would tie anklets with bells, and sing rapturous songs with a *kanjira* (a small, flat drum played with one hand white being held with the other) in hand. He revelled in songs of Kabir, Arabic songs and others through which he expressed his love. He had stopped his mighty dance at the Takia, but this trait lingered in him for decades. In 1910, when Rangri of Thana paid him a visit, Baba mentioned that the holy songs sung by the devotees the previous night had drowned him with overflowing love.

Baba refers to his obtaining the vision of God due to which He gave up the practice of herbal cures for diseases, administering only *udhi* (holy ash) and bestowal of grace. His self-absorption and meditative trance led him to *sakshatkara* or vision of God. He had various *siddhis* (supernatural powers) and could leave his body at will and return to it later. And the very faithful and true devotees who spent long hours in blissful communion with Baba had an extremely happy and painless death. A case in point is Mr. Dikshit, and an interesting narration is given about him.

Dikshit and Hemadpant (alias Anna Saheb Dhabolkar) went to Vile Parle to board a train. They were late by three minutes, but fortunately for them, the train also was late by three minutes. Having boarded the train and settled down in comfortable seats, Dikshit remarked how gracious it was of Baba to have delayed the train so that they could both board it. Soon Dikshit shut his eyes and the light went out of his life. Hemadpant, thinking him to be asleep, went to put cushions behind his back, but found him lifeless. His death was so peaceful, with words of gratitude for Baba during death, showing thereby that he had reached Baba.

Baba slept, for a large part of his life, on a plank that was suspended from the roof by flimsy strips of old cloth. It hung six feet above the ground, and some lamps were placed loosely on it. No doubt Baba levitated to get on to it, and to stay on it without breaking the flimsy ropes. His sleep, therefore, cannot have been a normal one. He was never in need of going into *samadhi* to attain a higher status or knowledge. He was always exercising a dual consciousness, one dealing with other egos in temporal or spiritual affairs, and the other abiding in the state of Universal Soul. He was forever exercising and exhibiting the powers and features of both states of consciousness. Unlike other states, he was always in the all-knowing state. Being in a state of permanent Divine Knowledge, normal sleep was not necessary for him. So Baba was not asleep at night but in a constant state of levitation and *samadhi*, keeping a vigil on his devotees and showering his grace upon them.

A Parsi lady, Mrs. Manager, says, "It was not merely his power that endeared him to his devotees. His loving care combined with the powers to make Shirdi a veritable paradise to those devotees who went there. Directly we arrived there we felt safe, that nothing could harm us. When I went and sat in his presence I always forgot my pain, and indeed the body itself and all mundane cares and anxieties. Hours would pass while I sat blissfully unaware of their passage. It was an extraordinary experience shared, I believe, by all his real devotees. He was all in All and the All of us."

Baba's influence had a purifying nature, as borne out by Y.J. Galwankar, "Once, when I went to Shirdi, in about 1917, Baba put his hand over my head, and this had a strange effect on me. I forgot myself and my surroundings and fell into a state of ecstasy. I learned afterwards that while I was in that state Sai Baba was telling those present that I was characterised by integrity and purity. He described to them various forms and conditions that I had passed through in previous lives and said that he had placed me in my mother's womb in this birth, and I had still retained my integrity and purity."

Sai Baba's love for his devotees was indeed great. He wielded great power over the elements, and saw that no harm befell the devotees through them. The following story bears testimony to it.

Once Hemadpant saw Sai Baba in silence! Soon the sky was overcast and dark, becoming darker as minutes ticked by. The birds and animals appeared stricken with fear. Soon a fierce gale was followed by heavy showers, a whirlwind, great commotion, thunder, lightning, and a squally wind. The showers turned to a very heavy downpour causing consternation and fear among the people and animals. The mosque soon became overcrowded, both inside and outside. Everything was soaking wet, crops, plants, people, animals and birds, rooftops, etc. Huddling together in fear, the people pleased with Baba to deliver them from the storm. As he fed on their sincere love and faith, he was moved to compassion. He rose from his seat, and standing on the raised front portion of the mosque, he roared to the gods in the highest pitch, so loud as to reverberate in the skies, and set even the mosque shaking. With his loud voice resounding, the rains gradually abated, the wind receded, and the sky cleared. Soon clusters of stars appeared in the sky, and the rain stopped completely. There was absolute peace in Shirdi, and even the animals and birds were at peace. The people thanked Baba profusely and returned to their homes. Such is Baba's kindness and greatness!

The following story will bear out how Baba controlled the fire. At midday, one day, the fire in the *dhuni* flared up suddenly, turning soon into an inferno, with the flames licking the rafters in the ceiling. Soon the mosque seemed to be in danger of being reduced to ashes. Yet Baba sat there, unruffled and at peace. People ran to fetch water to douse the fire, yet no one had the courage to pour it into the fire for fear of the *sataka* (baton) coming down heavily upon them. They were agitated and apprehensive, but lacked the courage to approach Baba.

Baba finally stirred, and picking up his *sataka*, he struck hard at the column that stood just at arm's length from the *dhuni.* He stared at the flame, saying, "Calm down, calm down!" With every stroke at the column, the fire, seemingly cowering, lost its fierceness, and soon the *dhuni* became calm. People heaved a sigh of relief, thanking Baba for ridding them of their fear. Baba, the compassionate, had once again answered their prayer.

Sai Baba was full of perfect joy, an incarnation of knowledge itself, being most sacred. He was the Perfect One, the destroyer of the fear of worldly life, and the propensities of all times. He created fear and dispelled it too, as one can see from the raging storm and fire, and then peace prevailing. A *darshan* of him always brought great joy and satisfaction. His company signified enjoyment of bliss as he liberated people from the fear of worldly life and created an awareness of a spiritual way of life.

4

Sai's Leelas

Sai is the Supreme Being of the universe, the benefactor, and the sole spirit of the existence. Never having read a book, he drew the best of learned scholars to him, and could explain to them the most complicated scriptural texts. He taught his devotees according to their own faith, yet made them live in peace together.

Sai taught us through a wild profusion of well-attested miracles. His miracles were flamboyant, as the following story depicts.

The nearest railway station to Kopergaon was some six miles from Shirdi, and the only conveyance was a horse carriage. Some devotees, who had come to Shirdi to see Baba, had to return urgently to Bombay, but there was a raging storm then. Sai Baba looked up at the sky and shouted, "Hey! Enough of that! Stop it now! My children have to go back." No sooner said than the storm stopped! But there was a purpose in his miracles. He said, "I give my devotees what they want so that they will begin to want what I want to give them."

Nanasaheb Chandorkar, a great devotee of Baba, was threatened with imminent death. "Nana is about to die, but will I let him?" said Baba. Nana and Lela Shastri were travelling in a *tonga* which suddenly overturned and they were both thrown to the ground. Baba, knowing the grave danger they were in, exercised his *siddhi* of saving them, and thus they were saved from death.

Nandram Marwadi of Shirdi, from whose house Baba begged for food every day, caught the plague infection that was epidemic there at that time. Baba assured him that he would not allow him to die till his own body perished. And thus Nandram continued to live for several decades.

When Buty came to Baba with the message that an astrologer had predicted danger of death of Buty on a particular day, Baba said, "What! Does he say that death will attack you? Strike. Let me see how you strike and kill." That day, a snake came near Buty, but slithered away without harming him. This ability of Baba to say that death shall not come to a person is distinctly divine. And so many devotees, like Tarabhai Sadashiv Tarkhad, always felt safe and that nothing could hurt them so long as they were in Baba's presence. They also felt Bliss radiating from Baba, permeating them for hours on end, like those experienced by Naryanashram, G. S. Khaparde, the South African doctor, and others.

Baba could leave his body at will and return to it

after a lapse of days, as borne out by Mahlsapati, who was witness to such an event. Baba left his body for three days then. In 1916, Baba looking very frail and weak, looked like death was imminent to him, but he declared that his *Seemolangan* (crossing the border) was the Dussera day two years hence. He drew his devotees to himself at the time of their deaths, though they may be thousands of miles away from Shirdi, and placed them in the best situations for their next birth. Such fortunate people were Rohilla, Babu Pradhan, Galwankar, Saptanekar's child, etc.

Baba could be present in two places at the same time, as is evident by the tale narrated by Mrs. Tarkhad. While she and her son were at Shirdi in Baba's company, he said that he had gone to their Bandra house to partake of the sugar-candy *naivedya* (offering) that was offered to him every day after *puja*. Not finding the offering there, he had returned hungry to Shirdi. Mr. Tarkhad, in his haste to go to office, had forgotten to offer *naivedya* to Sai after the *puja*, and when he remembered it rather late, he wrote to his wife about this great omission. But Mrs. Tarkhad had never felt the absence of Baba from Shirdi. This proves his presence everywhere at the same time.

Sai always appreciated love from his devotees and took immense trouble to have an ever vigilant eye on his devotees, always ensuring their welfare. This loving universal watch at all times was indeed divine, for when Dikshit forgot to offer the betel leaves and nuts for *naivedya* during his *puja* at home, Baba asked him to hand them over to him to make his *puja* complete, when Dikshit met him later at the mosque.

Baba's watchful eyes always discerned his devotees' wrongs, for he was always in a wakeful state. When people, intending to give a certain sum, paid only a part of it, Baba asked for the remainder. A woman, who decided to give eight annas as *dakshina* but finally gave only four annas to Baba, was told by him, "Why are you cheating Me ? Pay me the remaining four annas also". He could easily look into people's minds, being omniscient.

Baba always exuded bliss, which filled some of his devotees with a strange feeling of ecstasy, something which did not result from external or internal contact with any object of the senses but which completely gave the heart its highest satisfaction. A South African doctor, a Brahmin, came to Sai Baba without full faith in him. He hesitated to enter the mosque. But when his friend persuaded him to make at least one visit, he complied. And he suddenly rushed inside the mosque and fell at Baba's feet in total surrender. When questioned about this strange behaviour, he said, "I am a Rama devotee, but have had no personal or direct knowledge of Rama, but when I saw Baba, I saw in him my Rama for the first time, all the qualities of Rama in him. I found he was Neelamegha Shyama Rama, my *Ishta Devata*, and so I bowed to him gratefully." Since he considered Baba as Rama, he decided he would not go to the mosque again till Baba granted him his heart's desire — the perfect bliss of *Sat-chit-ananda* (Existence-Knowledge-Bliss). So he stayed away from the mosque for three days.

On the fourth day, while he was talking to an old friend, he forgot his vow, and in his friend's company went to see Baba. As they fell at his feet, Baba asked the doctor kindly, "Did anyone send for you?" The doctor felt ashamed, but seeing that Baba knew the secrets of his heart, he knew that he would grant him his desire, and Baba did! Baba being perfectly free from desires, totally self-controlled and always dwelling upon God, must certainly be immersed in *Satchitananda.*

Baba's powers over the mental state of his devotees were used by him to confer happiness of the highest level known to us—freedom from all miseries and physical pains and ailments. Mrs. Tarkhad states that when she sat before Baba with all her pains and worries, she felt them all leave her, keeping her in a joyful state. A Parsi, named happy state in Baba's presence. When he went to the mosque, his mind was full of worries concerning his sister's marriage and getting his insane brother cured. But on stepping into the mosque where Baba sat, the feeling of happiness washed over him in waves, leaving him devoid of anything else. Even when Baba appeared in his dreams, he had the same happy sensation.

Baba had the great power to see or hear things far from where he resided, for he was all-pervading and omnipresent. Without seeing and hearing he had the power to know, for his nature was pure *chit* (knowledge), and his power of divine vision enabled him to see or hear at the same time what transpired at different places, and thus make use of this knowledge for the benefit of his devotees. This was experienced by Kaka Mahajani who narrated the following story.

Kaka Mahajani's master's son, Sait, was discussing with Mahajani about his health. He wanted him to find out from Baba whether he should continue to stay at Nasik or not, with his health problems. Mahajani immediately suggested writing to Dikshit at Shirdi to do the needful, but Sait was vehement in his stand that Mahajani should do this personally.

While this discussion was going on at Nasik, Baba at Shirdi was telling Dikshit, "What talk is going on there? What deliberation?" Though Baba knew exactly what was happening miles away, yet Dikshit was bewildered by Baba's remarks. When Mahajani came to Baba the following day, Baba informed Dikshit that he was referring to this particular visit of Mahajani. On comparing notes, Mahajani and Dikshit realised Baba's divine powers of vision and illumination.

Baba could assume various forms to fit various occasions, as narrated by some of his devotees. He could take on any form or body, and had the ability to go anywhere and assume any form that he wished to. Nachne saw Sai Baba in an unfamiliar form when he came to the hospital to see his brother. He saw him in his house in yet another form, while the third form was of the *fakir* at the mosque.

Balakrishna Upasani Shastri states that he met a *sadhu* (ascetic) near a *tapovan* in Haridwar, who told him of his connections with his family in an earlier birth, using certain Hindustani phrases, meaning that there were two persons on a branch, one went up and another came down. When Balakrishna met Baba at Shirdi, Baba identified himself as the *sadhu* he had met at the *tapovan*, by using the same Hindustani phrase. On enquiry, Balakrishna found out that Baba had not left Shirdi even for a day to go to *tapovan!*

Balasaheb Deo, a very great Sai devotee, had a firm, unwavering faith in Baba. Once, he invited Baba for the *udyapan* dinner through a letter addressed to Jog. The *udyapan* (a ceremony concluding any religious observance) was being conducted as his mother's various vows had been fulfilled, and it was in the nature of gratitude to God that she was holding it at Dahanu. Jog informed him what Baba had said, "You, me and a third one, we three shall go together. Send him such a letter." Deo was absolutely thrilled, but wondered how Baba, who never went to any place outside Shirdi, with the exception of Rahata, Rui or Nungaon, would come so far as Dahanu.

A month before this invitation, a *Sanyasi* had come to Dahanu to collect contribution to improve the condition of an institution for cows. Deo told him to come to him after two or four months, as it was not feasible to grant him a huge sum of money then. The *sanyasi* went away quietly.

The day of the *udyapan* dawned. Just as preparations for the meal were going on, Deo suddenly espied the *sanyasi* outside his house. Suspicion arose at once, and he told his son, "This is the same *sanyasi* who had approached me earlier, and he has come for the contribution much before his time. Has he forgotten our conversation?" The *sanyasi* approached Deo, and seeing his restlessness, said, "I am not impatient for the money. It is a meal that we want today." Deo was relieved and told him to join the others at mealtime. Suddenly, the *sanyasi* said, "I have two boys with me." Deo invited them also, and then asked, "Where are you staying? Where can I send someone to call for you?" Baba said, "Where is the need for that? When should I come?" Deo told him to be present with the other two boys at twelve o'clock.

The *sanyasi* left, and returned with the boys exactly at twelve o'clock. They sat down to the meal and enjoyed it thoroughly. They left after the hearty meal with others. Deo wrote a letter to Jog accusing Baba of not keeping his promise to attend the *udyapan* meal. When Baba was narrated the full content of Deo's letter, he cried out in astonishment, "He says that after assuring him of the truth of my words I deceived him. Tell him that if he did not recognise me, why did he invite me? I had said that I would come accompanied by two others and so I had gone with the two. Seeing that I had come unexpectedly, was he not afraid that I would ask for money? And then I cleared his doubts. Did I not say that I will come only for the meal, bringing two others with me, and then came at the proper time with the two, and had lunch?" When Jog heard this, he was extremely happy and conveyed all this to Deo in a detailed letter. Deo's eyes filled with tears of love and joy, and he felt ashamed for having failed to recognise Sai.

Baba was the *Atman* or Soul who resides in all beings. He was the Supreme, permeating the universe, with His immanence in and transcendence of the universe. Baba once asked Chandorkar to bring *poli* (a sweet pancake) for *naivedya.* When they were placed before Baba, ants and flies settled on them, but Baba just sat there quietly, watching the *poli.* Then when He said that He had eaten them and Chandorkar might remove the plates, Chandorkar could hardly believe that Baba had eaten at all, for had he not sat there just watching the *poli?* Baba declared that he was the Soul of the ants and flies which had feasted on the *poli.* Chandorkar wanted proof, and when Baba raised his hands and made some gestures, Chandorkar realised that Baba knew the secrets of his heart and so must be his Soul too, and therefore the Soul of all beings.

When Hansraj was suffering from asthma, one day

he saw a cat eat all the curds, and so had beaten it. But it was Baba, in the form of a cat, who had saved Hansraj by eating the curds, for he had instructed Hansraj to avoid curds which was not good for his asthma. To prove that he had been beaten, he showed the weal on his shoulder.

Baba's control of the five elements was supreme. Once Megha had brought a pot of water from River Godavari, for Baba's bath. He was to have sprinkled only a few drops of water over Baba's head, yet in his enthusiasm he overturned the full pot of water over Baba's head. But to Megha's amazement, the water just wet Baba's head and nothing else.

Another incident involved M.W. Pradhan who wished to set out from Shirdi. The rains were pouring down heavily, and the Shirdi-Kopergaon road was flooded, preventing the plying of *tongas*. Pradhan feared that in such a condition, Baba would not permit him to leave Shirdi. But Baba uttered loudly, "O God, stop the rain. My children wish to go home." Soon the rains stopped, the water receded from the road, and Pradhan was able to set out on his journey.

Baba always ensured the safety of his loved ones. One evening, around seven o'clock, Shama was suddenly bitten by a snake on his little finger, the poison causing acute pain. Shama was in agony with pain and worry, and his whole body turned red. His friends begged him to go to the Vithoba temple since his life was in danger. His uncle suggested that he first take *udhi* and then go to the temple. Shama rushed to the mosque.

When he came up to Baba, the latter met his eyes and began abusing and cursing, not allowing him to come up the steps. He shouted, "Do not climb up. If you dare climb up, just beware! Get out, at once! Climb down and be gone!" Shama was stunned to see Baba so angry, breathing fire and fury. He panicked, and in a daze, sat down. He felt that Baba had rejected him and that all hope of a cure was lost. He felt like a lost child, bereft of its mother's arms.

After a while, Baba calmed down, and Shama, taking courage, went up to him and sat down. Baba said to him, "Do not lose courage, and have no worry whatsoever in your mind. All will be well. Give up worrying." He then ordered him to go home and sit quietly, asking him not to go out of the house, but have trust in him. He then sent Tatya Kote with a message, telling him to see that Shama did not sleep, and that he kept walking about in the house itself. And thus, Shama was saved from a poisonous death. Such indeed is the compassion of Sai, whose heart is kindled by love and compassion for his devotees. Shama later realised that the harsh words that Baba uttered were addressed to the poison, and not to him.

A Marwadi had a young daughter aged about eight years, who was stricken with palsied legs. Since she could not walk, she was carried in a chair to Baba. She remained with Baba for three days. Suddenly she found that she could bend and stretch her legs. On the following day, she found that she could stand, and soon she was able to walk. She was not given any medication or application, but the cure was purely by Baba's blessings and the smearing of *udhi* on her.

Another patient was suffering from inflammation of ulcers in the stomach for a long period. He was brought to Baba who ordered one of his devotees to buy some sweatmeats. When they were placed before the patient, he found to his delight that he could eat them with no sign of pain in his stomach, for he was completely cured by the grace and blessings of Baba.

Baba's pure divine blessings did wonders to all ailing people who sought his blessings. Bhagoji Shinde was afflicted with leprosy as a result of the great sins of his past life. His body was fall of bleeding sores, the toes and fingers having fallen off due to the advanced stage of leprosy. The whole body exuded a repulsive stench, yet he was very dear to Baba.

One day, Baba was sitting near the *dhuni*, adding logs into the fire. Suddenly, he thrust his hand in the fire, keeping it in the fire, quite unaware of pain. Shama, noticing this, ran instantly to Baba, and putting his arms around his waist, as he stood behind Baba, he quickly pulled him back, shouting, "Baba, what have you done?" Baba instantly came back to awareness, and said, "Oh, Shama, a child slipped from its mother's arms into the smith's forge, for she had been blowing the bellows vigorously and had forgotten about the child in her arms. As I was picking her up, this is what happened! Let the hand be scorched, yet at least the child's life is saved!" And who else, but Bhagoji alone had the privilege of massaging Baba's hand with *ghee* (clarified butter), covering it with a leaf, and bandaging it tightly. People were concerned that Baba would contact leprosy from Bhagoji, but far from it!

One day, in the early years of his life at Shirdi, Baba was grinding wheat on the quern that was placed on a sack, his legs spread out, his hands rotating the quern-stone with a handle on it. Everyone was amazed at such a sight, and soon people gathered to see what was happening. Four women immediately seized hold of Baba's hand, and quickly took his place in grinding the wheat, without heeding his protests. They sang Baba's praises as they did so. Baba's mock anger gave way to love and tenderness, a smile brightening his face.

When the grinding of the wheat was completed, the four women decided that since Baba was alone, he did not need all that wheat flour. So they filled the scuttle basket with flour, preparing to take it to their homes. Baba watched all this silently. When the women started dividing the flour into four portions for themselves, Baba said in anger, "Are you out of your senses? Where are you taking the flour? Does it belong to your father that you are carrying it away? Go at once to the village boundary and throw all the flour at the side of the brook there! Freebooters all! How they come running to loot me! Was it some borrowed wheat that you now stake a claim to the flour?"

The women, ashamed of themselves, did as Baba commanded. Later, this strange act of Baba found a reasonable explanation. When Baba had started grinding, it was not the wheat but the terrible cholera epidemic that he fed to the quern to be crushed. Then by scattering the ground flour along the side of the brook at the village border, the epidemic started waning, and soon the village was free of the disease. Thus, by employing this mysterious remedy, Baba showed the people his *leela* and divine power.

Once, Das Ganu wished to go to Prayag for a dip in the holy Ganges. When he approached Baba for permission, Baba told him that Shirdi itself was Prayag, and this firm faith he should have in his mind. Das Ganu immediately obeyed, and to his wonder, as he placed his hand on Baba's feet, water trickled from both his toes, the waters of the Ganga and the Jamuna. Seeing this *leela*, Das Ganu was beside himself with sheer joy. He bowed to Baba with tears of gratitude and love. No doubt people go to the Ganges to wash away their terrible sins, while the river herself takes refuge at Sainath's feet to cleanse her own self!

Baba knew the past, the present and the future. Once Nana Saheb had to leave for Pandharpur, for he was transferred there. But before going there he wanted to have a *darshan* of Baba. Since he had to join duty quickly, he left in a hurry for Shirdi with his family. No one expected him, but Baba knew of his arrival. Baba suddenly started singing a *bhajan*.

To Pandharpur I go, I go
There alone do I stay
There alone do I stay, I stay
In that abode of my Lord!

The devotees too joined in singing this refrain, when suddenly Nana arrived. Bowing at Baba's feet, he along with his family, sought Baba's grace, entreating him to accompany them to Pandharpur and remain there. The people assured him about Baba's interest in going there and told of the *bhajan* that they sang. Baba's *leela* astonished him, and with great reverence and choking with emotion, he placed his head on Baba's feet. After taking his blessings and *udhi* he left for Pandharpur.

Baba was always watching all that was going on around him. His love and compassion for all living creatures was unique. One day, one of his ardent devotees was serving food to her family when suddenly a hungry dog came in. She gave a quarter of the *bhakari* from her plate to it. Then came a dirty pig, smeared all over with mud and filth. To it also she fed a piece of the *bhakari*. Soon she forgot all about this, as this came to her very naturally.

In the afternoon, when she sat in front of Baba at the mosque, he told her affectionately that her feeding him that day had appeased his acute hunger. "That is what you should always do. For truly, this alone will stand you in good stead. . . . Always have compassion. First feed those who are hungry, then eat yourself. Preserve this truth carefully in your heart."

The lady wondered what exactly Baba meant. So she asked him, "How is it possible that I have given you food? I myself depend on others and eat whatever I get." Baba reminded her that she had first fed a hungry dog, then a filthy pig, and that Baba is one with them. He said, "Sometimes I am a dog and sometimes a pig; sometimes I am a cow, a cat, an ant, a fly — in various forms do I move in this world." He stated that whoever saw him in all living beings was dear to him. He advised her that the way to worship him was to give up all sense of differentiation. The lady felt ecstatic in Baba's presence after hearing these nectar-like words.

Baba was all-pervasive, and was one with his devotees also. Once Purandare, another devotee, came to Shirdi, carrying with him brinjals sent by Mrs. Tarkhad for Baba. She instructed Purandare's wife to prepare *bharit* (brinjal roasted and seasoned) with half the brinjals, and the remaining to be sliced and fried crisply. These were then to be offered to Baba.

Mrs. Purandare prepared the *bharit*, and after offering *naivedya* to God, she left the plate of *bharit* for Baba and went home. Baba sat down to his meal, after collecting the *naivedyas* offered by different people. He enjoyed the *bharit* very much, and asked for the fried brinjals. Everyone thought that he was asking for them as he had enjoyed the *bharit.* But there was a problem. Brinjals were not in season, so from where could they fetch them? They remembered that Mrs. Purandare had prepared the *bharit,* and probably she had some more brinjals with her.

When the people approached her with Baba's request, she told them that she had sliced the brinjals and was planning to try them later and offer them to Baba. Later, they all realised, after piecing together the full story, what Mrs. Tarkhad's instructions had been—to serve both at the same time—and that Baba had known about this!

In 1915, on another occasion, Balram Mankar's son was on his way to Shirdi to perform the last rites of his recently expired father. He went to Mrs. Tarkhad's house to tell her about his plans. She wanted to send something for Baba, but not finding anything other than a single *peda* that had already been offered as *naivedya,* she decided to send it to Baba, knowing he would relish it.

The boy carried the single *peda* to Shirdi, with the promise that he would give it to Baba with Mrs. Tarkhad's love. When he went to Baba for his *darshan,* he forgot to take the sweet with him to the mosque. Baba was patient with him. When again he went to see Baba, yet again he forgot all about the *peda.* Baba asked him, "What have you brought for me?" When the boy said that he had nothing with him, Baba reminded him gently, "Has no one given you anything for me?" He again replied in the negative. Then Sai asked him directly, "My boy, did not mother very lovingly send with you some sweet for me, when you left home?" It was only then that he remembered. He was deeply mortified and hung his head in shame. Running to his lodge, he fetched the *peda* and handed it over to Baba who quickly ate it with great relish. Baba, who sat in the mosque at Shirdi knew what happened elsewhere in the world.

Inscrutable are Sai's innumerable *leelas*. Though some people or devotees do not know their own welfare, Baba knows it very clearly. Once, Bhausaheb Dhumal, a renowned lawyer of Nasik, came to Shirdi to have Baba's *darshan*. His plan was to return immediately after the *darshan*, alighting at Niphad for a court case. But Baba willed it otherwise.

When Dhumal asked Baba's permission to leave Shirdi, Baba refused. He detained him for a week, refusing permission in no uncertain terms. The case too got postponed. Then Baba made him stay for another few days. During this time, the judge suffered an acute colic due to which the hearing was adjourned. For Dhumal, it was a very rewarding time in Baba's presence, free from anxiety and worry, for he reposed full faith in Baba. And his total faith in Baba led to his getting an acquittal for his client.

Then there is the tale that Mahajani recounted to Hemadpant later on. He once travelled from Bombay to

Shirdi, hoping to spend a week there, and participate in the Gokulashtami celebrations there. When he went to Baba for his *darshan,* Sai said, "So when do you return home?" Kaka was taken aback, and thought, "Why this question the moment I met him?" But, he answered humbly, "Whenever Baba gives me the command, I shall return home." Baba told him to return the following day and Kaka obeyed quietly.

When Kaka reached Bombay, he found that the managing clerk had suddenly taken ill, and Kaka's presence was needed urgently, and his employer said that he had sent him a letter to this effect, asking him to return immediately. This shows Baba's vision of the present and the future.

Once, Mulay, a rigid ritualistic Agnihotri Brahmin, came to Shirdi from Nasik, by virtue of his accumulated past merit. He had come to meet Shrimant Bapusaheb Buty, and planned to leave Shirdi immediately after. After meeting him, as Mulay and others got up to go to the mosque, he too felt a desire to joint them. So he accompanied them to the mosque.

Mulay was a great scholar, well-versed in the *Shastras,* astrology and palmistry. He was thrilled to have Baba's *darshan.* Baba was distributing the basketful of bananas to all the devotees. When Mulay bowed at Baba's feet, he was fascinated by them and had a great desire to read the lines and signs of his feet. Somebody introduced Mulay to Baba, and requested Baba to give him *prasad* also. But Baba had his own mind and, indeed, who could force him? Anyway, Mulay was not interested in the fruits, only to read the lines on Baba's palm now. He stretched out his own hand to take Baba's hand in his, but Baba ignored him and continued distributing the fruit. Mulay pleaded with Baba, but he was stubbornly ignoring him. He placed four bananas in his hand, but refused to show his hand.

Mulay finally gave up all efforts, and sat quietly for a time, then returned to the *wada* with others, where he began his ritual of maintaining the perpetual fire. Baba set out for the Lendi, suggesting that they all wear ochre-coloured robes that day, and carry an ochre chalk with them. People were surprised by this strange suggestion, but they did as ordered.

Baba returned from the Lendi to the mosque amidst the sounds of kettledrums, horns, etc. Bapusaheb Jog told Mulay that it was time for the *arati*, and was he coming? An awkward Mulay suggested coming there later in the afternoon.

Baba was seated in the mosque, and the people had offered the *puja*, waiting now for the *arati*. Suddenly, Baba said, "Go, bring *dakshina* from that Brahmin who has just arrived." Bapusaheb Buty set out to collect the *dakshina*. Mulay was sitting in yoga, after his bath, with a calm and steady mind. When he heard Baba's request of *dakshina*, doubts assailed him, "Why should I give *dakshina?* I am a pure Brahmin. Baba may be a great saint, but I am not beholden to him in any way! Why should I pay him *dakshina?*" Then he also felt that a great saint like Baba had asked for it through a millionaire, and he decided to give *dakshina* to Baba at the mosque.

As he came to the mosque, another doubt had his steps faltering. He was pure in body and mind, while the mosque was visited by people from all communities. Since he had not yet completed his ritual, he felt he could not enter the mosque. So, from a distance, he showered flowers on Baba with the palms cupped together. And then, right in from of him a miracle took place. Baba disappeared, and in his seat sat his revered guru, Gholapnath, who had already taken *samadhi* long ago. Mulay stood there, amazed and speechless, his mind washed of all doubts, leaving it clear, with the awareness that Baba was beyond all powers of reasoning. He rushed forward at once and embraced his feet. When he looked up it was Baba that he was prostrating to. He felt pride melting away, his eyes being purified with the knowledge that he had met his guru, the Light Eternal, and his soul was blessed with the treasure of knowledge. With half-closed eyes he stood gazing at Baba's sacred feet, his love for Baba gushing out from his very being.

People wondered at the transformation in Mulay, who till then, had been offering flowers to Baba from a distance, and was now clinging to his feet. Later they understood the significance of Baba's ochre clothes and chalk, for Gholapnath had appeared in ochre robes with the ochre mark on his forehead. But who can truly understand Baba's mysterious *leelas*?

There is another wonderful experience that occurred to a doctor, a great Rama devotee. A devotee set out to Shirdi, taking with him his doctor friend. The doctor was reluctant to pay obeisance to a Muslim *fakir*, for he considered himself to be a strict follower of the rites, rituals, etc., as prescribed by the *Shastras*. But the devotee assured him that no one would force him to touch Baba's feet, and that he had only to make up his mind firmly to go with him.

The doctor pushed aside all doubts and set out to have Baba's *darshan*. When he arrived at the mosque for *darshan*, wonder of wonders, it was he who first prostrated before *Baba*! His friend gaped at him in sheer amazement. So he asked the doctor what had made him change his mind and prostrate before a Muslim. The doctor replied that he saw in Baba's place the vision of Shri Rama in his dark blue hue, seated with a serene smile on his face. As he bowed and raised his head, he saw Sai's figure in place of Rama. So he said, "How can I call this a dream? How can he be a Muslim? No, indeed! He is a yogi, an incarnate of God!"

His pride and egoism had evaporated. He vowed he would not step into the mosque again unless Baba blessed him. For three days he stood by his vow. On the fourth day, one of his friends whom he had not met for many years, suddenly arrived at Shirdi for Baba's *darshan*. Meeting him after a lapse of nine years, his joy knew no bounds, and he followed his friend to the mosque! He immediately made his obeisance to Baba, who then asked him, "So, doctor, did anyone come to call you? Then tell me first, why have you come?" Hearing this, the doctor was overcome with emotion, and regretted his resolve. But that night, during midnight, Baba blessed him with his grace, and the doctor tasted the sweetness of ecstasy! He returned to his village, but continued to experience that Pure Bliss for a fortnight! Such marvellous indeed are Baba's *leelas*.

Though outwardly Baba seemed to do nothing, and did not even leave his place, he knew everything and showed his *leelas* as proof of it to all the people. There is absolutely no doubt in anyone's mind that his whole creation, animate and inanimate, is pervaded by Sai. Anyone may experience it for himself, as a Parsi merchant named Ratanji discovered. He had immense wealth and extensive property, and his doors were always open to all. Amidst all this luxury, he was restless and sorrowful. He was extremely generous, and alleviated the sufferings of the needy. Though he appeared to be cheerful outwardly, he was sad that he had no children. When he expressed his deep longing for a child to Das Ganu, he was advised to go to Shirdi for Baba's *darshan*, and his wish would be fulfilled.

Accordingly Ratanji arrived at Shirdi. He went to the mosque and paid obeisance at Sai's feet. As he looked up at Baba, his eyes welled up with tears of joy and love. He took out a garland from his basket and put it lovingly around Baba's neck. He then offered him various varieties of fruits, and sat at his feet with great reverence. Then he said with great humility, "When people are in trouble, they come to Baba's feet, and he protects them immediately. Hence I have come all the way here, with an ardent wish. Please do not turn me away. Oh Maharaj!"

Baba replied, "And so after all these days, you have come to me today! But then, give me first, whatever *dakshina* you wish to give. Only then will you get your satisfaction." Now Sai asked for *dakshina* only for the good of his devotees. He was educating them in renunciation. He had no need of any *dakshina* for his subsistence. When Ratanji was about to take out the *dakshina* from his pocket, Baba said, "I know that you have already given me three rupees and fourteen annas. Now give me the remaining money which you have brought with you, as *dakshina*."

Ratanji was completely taken aback. What rupees and annas was he talking about? This was his first visit to Shirdi and *darshan* of Baba, so Baba's words were perplexing and beyond his comprehension. Yet, bowing at Baba's feet, he gave the *dakshina*, prostrated before him, then sat with folded hands, and prayed to Baba, "Baba, it was indeed my good fortune to have your *darshan* today. I am without much knowledge, but by my good fortune, I had today the *darshan* of one who knows the past, present and future, and is wise. You know my anxiety only too well. Remove it, Oh

Gracious One! Do not push this faithful devotee away from your feet, Oh All-Merciful One."

Moved by compassion, Baba blessed him, placing his hand of benediction on Ratanji's head, and said, "Allah will fulfil yours heart's desire." Taking permission, Ratanji returned to Nanded.

When he met Das Ganu, he narrated to him all that had transpired at the mosque in Shirdi, and how greatly satisfied he was with Baba's *darshan.* But there was one thing which was an enigma. "How could I have given anything to him before? This was my first visit to Shirdi. Oh, I do not understand the significance of this at all! Can you at least solve it for me?"

Das Ganu pondered over this for a long time. Suddenly he remembered a Muslim saint called Maulisaheb who worked as a porter. Before Ratanji left for Shirdi, Mauli had come to his house, for they had boundless love for each other. Ratanji had offered him flowers, fruits, etc., with proper ritual, and then offered him a light meal. When Das Ganu added up the expenses incurred on that day, he came up with the figure that Baba said Ratanji had spent on him — three rupees and fourteen annas! Ratanji realised at once that there was no separateness between Baba and Maulisaheb. Mauli's *Atman* was the same as that of all the others. Both were of the same Essence; their life-force was one. No doubt Shirdi was far from Nanded, but being one, this telegraphic message to each other was possible.

With suitable passage of time, Ratanji was blessed with children, and he carried offerings of various fruits for Baba. His son, afflicted with leprosy, soon recovered from it at Shirdi by Baba's grace.

As Pitale, a Sai devotee took leave of Baba after receiving the *udhi* from him, Baba suddenly took out three rupees from his pocket, and gave them to him, saying, "I had given you two rupees earlier; keep these three along with them and perform their *puja* regularly. It will benefit you greatly." Pitale accepted them happily as *prasad*, and prostrating before Baba, sought his blessings. But a sudden doubt leapt into his mind. This was his first trip to Shirdi, and his first *darshan* of Baba. So, when had he given him two rupees? His curiosity grew, but Baba did not seem to give any indication, and he went back to Bombay with a puzzled mind.

Pitale's mother was eager to hear about her son's visit to Shirdi. When he narrated everything, the subject that had been puzzling him came up. She too pondered upon it when suddenly she remembered an event of the past that solved the puzzle. She said, "Recently you took your son to Shirdi, so that he had Baba's *darshan*. Similarly, in the past, you father too had taken you to Akkalkot. The Maharaj there, known for his kindness and generosity, was an enlightened yogi. Your father too was pure and sinless. Pleased with the *puja* that your father offered, he gave two rupees as *prasad* to be worshipped in the daily *puja*. Your father performed the *puja* daily with great faith." She then said that they had been lost due to the carelessness of the children, but now he was fortunate to have met Akkalkot Maharaj himself in the form of Sai.

Pitale's heart was full of joy and love for Sai as he heard this narration. His devotion for Sai grew stauncher, and he realised that Sai had awakened him to a sense of duty.

Sai Baba's purpose in performing *leelas* was to establish a firm faith and belief in God, especially in adverse conditions, as Gopal Narayan Ambedkar found out. He had been serving in the excise department under the British government for ten years. Then he quit the job and sat at home. Due to adverse planetary situation, his fortunes changed for the worse. Though he tried to get some job, he had no luck. Gradually, his financial status started worsening, and soon calamities followed in rapid succession. Life at home became unbearable.

Seven years of such hardship passed, and every year he went to Shirdi, sat at Baba's feet, and poured out his sufferings. One day, he resolved to end his life, knowing fully that it was a sin to commit suicide, but he felt there was no redemption for him. He sat in a bullock-cart one night, in front of the Dikshit-wada, with the determination to jump into the well, and thus end his sufferings.

Just then, Sagun Meru Naik, a great devotee of Sai Baba, who ran an eating-house nearby, emerged from the door, and seeing Ambedkar, asked, "Have you read this *pothi* (book) of Akkalkot Maharaj?"

Ambedkar grabbed it eagerly, and leafing the pages quickly, suddenly stopped to read from somewhere in the middle of the book. What he read transformed his thoughts totally. One of Akkalkot Maharaj's devotees was suffering untold miseries and a disease that was not curable. Now he could bear the pain no longer, and so he determined to end his life. At night, when everything was quiet, he went to a well and jumped into it. Suddenly Maharaj fished him out with his own hands, and said to him, "Whatever suffering fate has ordained for us, one has to bear. Unless we fully suffer the consequences of our previous *karma*, in the form of disease, affliction, leprosy or pain, what can a suicide do? Unless this pain and suffering is undergone fully another birth has to be taken to complete it. Therefore, bear this suffering a little more. Do not be provoked into destroying your own life."

Ambedkar realised that this story coincided so much with his own present situation that he felt quite ashamed of his cowardice in the face of such all-pervasiveness of Baba. On seeing Sai's marvellous *leela*, his faith in Sai strengthened double-fold, and by Sai's grace and *udhi*, his troubles started waning. As his devotion to his guru grew, happiness and prosperity followed and he soon grew to be a very devoted, contented and happy follower of Sai.

Sai's *leela* is like a wish-fulfilling tree, bearing fruits and flowers which can be plucked only by a fortunate devotee. One of them happened to be such a fortunate one. He was Kakaji Vaidya, living in the village of Vani in Nasik district, and working as a priest in the temple of Goddess Saptashrungi. He was unhappy with life, his mind always distressed by the miseries of worldly life. He begged the goddess to free him from the worries and anxieties that troubled him.

The goddess, pleased with his devotion, appeared before him in a dream, and said, "Go to Baba, and your mind will be calm and steady." But before he could understand who this Baba was, he woke up.

He pondered over who this Baba could be, and decided that he must be Tryambakeshwar (Shiva — the reigning deity of the temple of that name). So he set out immediately, and had the *darshan* of the Lord there. Yet his mind continued to be agitated and restless. He spent ten days there, but found no steadying of mind. Reluctantly he returned to Vani.

Every morning at dawn, he would bathe, then recite the *Rudra*, a *mantra* from the *Yajurveda*, in praise of Shiva, and offer puja to the *Shivalinga*, but he found no solace. Again he went to the temple of the goddess, and cried out piteously, "Why did you send me to Tryambakeshwar? Please spare me these journeys which do not soothe my restless mind."

Taking pity on him, the goddess appeared in a vision that night, saying, "The Baba I mentioned is Sai Samarth of Shirdi. Why did you needlessly go to

Trymbakeshwar?"

Kakaji lamented the fact that he did not know where Shirdi was, how one could get there, who this Baba was, or how this trip to Shirdi would materialise. But he need not have worried, for Sai has his own ways of granting *darshan* to the truly devoted and faithful person. He sent as a messenger, Madhavrao, whom he loved better than all, whose love for Baba was beyond comparison, and whose authority too was very great. They would frequently have disputes, and address each other in a familiar way.

When Madhavrao was a child, he fell ill, and his mother had offered him to the goddess, Saptashrungi, telling her to take care of him, and if he recovered, then she would place him at her feet. She suffered from boils on her breasts, and the suffering was agonising. She promised to offer the goddess two silver breasts at her feet if her pain was relieved. Once her son recovered from the illness, and her boils disappeared she forgot all about her vows. As she was on her death-bed, she remembered her promises to the goddess, and entreated Madhavrao to fulfil them, before she left the world.

Madhavrao too gradually forgot about this, and thirty years lapsed uneventfully. An astrologer happened to visit Shirdi one day, and meeting Madhavrao's brother, Bapaji, who wanted his future to be predicted, he said, "Your mother had asked your elder brother to fulfil her vows at the time of her death. They have not yet been fulfilled, and so the goddess is giving you your problems."

When Madhavrao heard this, he felt repentant, and had two silver breasts made by the goldsmith. Taking these to the mosque, he placed them before Baba and said, "You are our Saptashrungi; you are the goddess for us. Please accept this promised gift, and be pacified."

Baba told him to go personally to Vani and offer them to the goddess with his own hands. He took Baba's *darshan*, prayed for his blessings, and taking the *udhi*, set out for Vani. There, he began to search for the family priest, and who should he meet, but Kakaji. Here was Kakaji, waiting for Baba's *darshan*, and Baba's messenger was before him! This surely could not be an ordinary, commonplace occurrence!

When Kakaji realised that Madhavrao had come from Shirdi, he was beside himself with joy. He took him to the temple where Madhavrao offered the silver breasts at the feet of the goddess, thus completing the ritual for fulfilling the vows. They then quickly left for Shirdi, with love and eagerness filling their hearts.

When Kakaji saw Baba, he made obeisance at his feet, bathing them with the tears of joy and love that welled up in his eyes. He at once felt his mind becoming calm and happy, and his heart's wish fulfilled. He marvelled at Sai's *leela;* not a word had

Baba spoken to him, not asked him any questions, yet his *darshan* had brought pure joy to his heart! As he surrendered himself to Baba with all faith and devotion, he experienced an inner bliss. He spent twelve days in Shirdi thus, and returned to Vani with a peaceful and happy mind.

Then there is the tale of how Khushalbhau experienced Sai's *leela*. One day Baba told Dikshit to go to Rahata and fetch Khushalbhau in a *tonga*, as he felt a great desire to meet him. When Dikshit reached his house in a *tonga*, great was Khushalbhau's surprise. He said that he had just then woken up from sleep, and had dreamt that Baba was ordering him to come to Shirdi immediately. He too felt a strange urge to see Baba, but since his horse was not there, he had sent his son to inform Baba. So he was all the more surprised to see Dikshit with the *tonga*. He went immediately with Dikshit to Shirdi, and was very pleased to meet Baba whose wish too was satisfied. Khushalbhau was overcome with emotion on seeing Baba's *leela*.

Baba brought people to Shirdi to fulfil their wishes, to have his *darshan*, and thus satisfy their worldly and spiritual ends. Ramlal was thus drawn to Shirdi by Baba's grace. He was a Punjabi Brahmin, living in Bombay. He had an extraordinary dream in which Baba said, "Come to visit me." Ramlal had not seen this great saintly figure before. He wanted to go and meet him, but he did not know his place or address. But Baba, who had called him, had his own ways of bringing devotees to himself.

As Ramlal was walking on the road in the afternoon, he was startled to see the picture of the saint who had appeared in his dream. He rushed to the shopkeeper and enquired, "Who is he? Where does he belong?" When he was told that the picture was of Shirdi Sai Baba, he was satisfied. Later, after finding out all the details of how to reach Shirdi, he went there and stayed on with Baba till Sai attained *samadhi*.

How unfathomable and incomprehensible is Sai's *leela*, and so boundless his favour. Once two gentlemen from Goa came to Shirdi for Sai's *darshan*. Delighted by this *darshan*, they sat at his feet, totally engrossed in the happiness they got from his presence. Though they had come together, Baba asked only one of them to give a *dakshina* of fifteen rupees, which was given happily and immediately. Though the other was not asked for a *dakshina*, he volunteered to give thirty-five rupees which Baba promptly refused.

Shama (alias Madhavrao), who was watching this, asked Sai, "Baba, how can you do this? When they have come together, you ask for *dakshina* from one, and when the other offers, you refuse. How can you differentiate thus?"

Baba replied, "Shama, you do not understand! I, for one, never take anything from anyone. It is the Presiding Goddess who asks for her dues, by paying which the giver is freed of his debt. People make vows before goddesses when in need, but I have to take the trouble to free them from the goddesses."

Then Baba narrated the following story. This man, from whom Baba had asked for *dakshina*, had been very poor initially. He made a vow to the goddess that if he earned fifteen rupees, he would offer his first income to her. When he did earn such a sum, he forgot his vow. The salary kept multiplying, till he began earning Rs.700 per month. By a wonderful union of his destiny and good work, he had come to Shirdi that day, and so Baba asked him for the fifteen rupees that he had vowed he would offer to the goddess, as *dakshina*.

Then Baba narrated another story. "Once, as I was wandering along the seacoast, I came across a huge mansion. As I went to it, I was cordially invited by the wealthy Brahmin residing there. He offered me food and drink in plenty. Then he gave me a comfortable place, near an inbuilt cupboard, to sleep.

"While I slept, the Brahmin broke open the wall by sliding a stone slat. Then he cut open my pocket, from which he stole the thirty thousand rupees that were there. When I awoke, to my horror, I found all my wealth gone. My mind was greatly agitated, and the Brahmin, pretending to be sincere and honest, tried to pacify me. I could neither enjoy my food nor my sleep, sitting in the veranda, a picture of abject misery.

"After a fortnight, a *fakir*, wandering on the road, suddenly appeared before me, and seeing me weeping, asked me the reason. I told him everything in detail. He told me to do as he instructed, and all my troubles would end. He suggested that I meet the *fakir* about whom he would furnish details, and surrender to him wholeheartedly, so that I would be able to recover all that had been stolen. But there was a condition too — I had to give up an item of food that I was very fond of, till I had accomplished my object. By following the instructions, I met the *fakir* as suggested and recovered my money. I then left the mansion and went along the seacoast as before.

"Eventually I found a boat, but was not allowed to board it. Suddenly, a good-natured *sepoy*, who arrived there, found a place for me on the boat, and I reached the other shore in time. Then, taking a *tonga*, I came home." Thus ended Baba's tale, and he commanded Shama to take the guests home and feed them.

When Shama told them that Baba had not known the sea, the boat or the sepoy, and that he had spent all his life at the foot of the tree in the mosque, and that he had no wealth that a thief could rob, the second person from Goa, choked with emotion, cried out, "Sai is all-knowing God-incarnate, who is one with God, invisible and all-pervasive. The stories that he narrated are true. But how did he know all this, when he does not even know us?"

The second person then narrated his story. A Brahmin had been in his service for thirty-five years, working diligently and trustfully. One day, unfortunately, he gave in to temptation. He slid the stones in the wall where the inbuilt cupboard was located, and made a hole without anyone's knowledge, just as Baba had mentioned. He then stole a bundle of notes amounting to thirty thousand rupees, and hid them.

As the Goan was lamenting the loss of all his wealth, after a fortnight, he saw a *fakir* walking up to him at the veranda. Seeing his sad face, the *fakir* asked him the reason. He suggested, after hearing everything, that he should visit Shirdi and pay homage to Sai Baba there, thus getting his grace and *darshan*. But till then he had to give up a favourite food item. This the Goan carried out to the letter. After a fortnight, the Brahmin who had stolen his money, returned his money of his own accord, asking forgiveness for letting his intellect betray him and commit a sin.

All went well after that. The Goan had a fond desire to visit Baba, and that too got fulfilled, with Baba's grace. Then he also told Shama, that having seen Baba in a dream, he set out for Shirdi. And all that Baba had described about the refusal of permission to enter the boat, and the averting of the difficulty by the *sepoy's* efforts were all true. He confessed that though the *sepoy* was a stranger to him, he said that he knew the Goan, and added, "Thinking of this marvel, my mind is simply nonplussed, and I realise that Sai fills this entire universe."

Hemadpant (Govind Raghunath Dabholkar —

Baba called him Hemadpant) once had a *darshan* of Baba in the beautiful dress of a *sanyasi*, where Baba said, "Today, I am coming for a meal." When he woke up, he realised it was a dream, but he remembered every detail distinctly. Filled with sheer joy, he told his wife in full faith, "Today is the festival of Holi. A guest is coming for lunch. Remember to cook a quarter seer more of rice." She asked in doubt, "Why will Baba come all the way from Shirdi?" He replied, "Even I do not say that Sai will personally be the guest, but I feel without doubt that somebody or other will come. You may then regard him as anyone you like, but to me he will be Sai. Or rather, I will regard him as none other than Sai, and thus my dream will come true."

At noon, *puja* was performed to the holy fire with proper rituals, and then plates were laid out for the meal to be served. Everyone sat down for the meal, and one place was reserved for Sai. They all waited for the guest to come, but how long should one wait, thought Hemadpant. Finally, food was served, and just as they were about to start eating, footsteps were heard rushing on the staircase, and someone shouting, "Where is Raosaheb?" The diners sat still.

Hemadpant opened the door, and two men stood outside. One of them was Ali Mohammed, the other was a disciple of Maulana Ismu Mujawar. Ali said, "Pardon me for interrupting the meal, and keeping the others waiting. So just take this thing, which is yours. I shall meet you later, and tell you in detail, the marvellous wonder about this." So saying, he took out from the newspaper wrapping a bas-relief of Sai. He handed it to Hemadpant reverentially. On seeing Sai in front of him in the form of a bas-relief, his throat choked with emotion, his heart surging with joy and love, eyes welling up with tears of sheer joy, for Sai had blessed him by showing his *leela*. Under this guise he had proved his words in Hemadpant's dream. Everyone was delighted to see the beautiful image of Sai in that bas-relief. With the picture occupying the pride of place with the diners, *puja* was performed with proper rites and rituals, and after *naivedya* was offered to Baba, the diners had the meal, relishing every bit of food cooked with such love and gratitude.

Ali Mohammed's tale of how he received Baba's bas-relief bears testimony to one of the most amusing *leelas* of Baba. He was walking along the road in Bombay one day when he came upon a bas-relief of Sai Baba. Being greatly attracted to it, he purchased it and hung it on a wall along with the pictures of other Muslim saints in his house.

Three months before he parted with the picture, he fell very ill, with one of his legs swollen, which had to be operated upon. He stayed with his brother-in-law, Noormohammed Peerbhoy during these three months.

A small picture of Baba Abdul Raheman, given to Ali by Mohammed Hussein, hung on the wall with the other pictures in Ali's house. One such copy was also with his brother-in-law, lying in the drawer of his table for eight years. Once he chanced upon it, and taking it to a studio, got a fine print made out of it. He decided to take it to Baba Abdul himself and present it to him expecting him to be pleased and overwhelmed with love. He got copies made from it, and distributed them to very close relatives.

When people gathered at the assembly which was being graced by Abdul Raheman, Peerbhoy presented the picture to him. On seeing the picture and realising his intention, Abdul Raheman was furious and rose to beat him. Driven away after being treated with indignity, Peerbhoy became agitated in mind, feeling dejected, humbled and sad. He realised that keeping the pictures of saints in the house was objectionable, and thus he had incurred his guru's wrath, and thereby lost his love. So he destroyed the picture by immersing it in water, and then threw the whole lot into the sea. He went round his relatives' house to collect those which he had distributed, and likewise destroyed them. He advised Ali also to destroy all pictures, for he was sure they brought calamities and his illness.

Ali called his assistant and asked him to fetch all the pictures of saints hung on the wall, and entrust them to Peerbhoy to be destroyed, which was promptly carried out.

When Ali returned to his house after two months, he was astonished to see the bas-relief of Sai still on the wall. He did not want it destroyed, so he hid it for some time, but the fear of its being found made him worried. He wanted to present it to a man worthy of it, who would revere it and do *puja* to it every day. Sai himself inspired a good idea in him, and so he went to Maulana Mujawar Ismu and confessed everything to him. According to his suggestion, he brought it to Hemadpant on Holi festival just as everyone was ready to eat the meal. No doubt Sai's oneness with all things, animate and inanimate, and his ingenuity, are inconceivable!

Another fascinating story about Balasaheb Deo lends credence to the magnificence of Baba's *leela*. Deo wished to read the *Jnaneshwari* regularly every day, but due to some obstacle or another, he could not fulfil his wish. He read the *Bhagavad Gita* without any hindrance, but to read even one chapter of the *Jnaneshwari* brought some obstacle. He went to Shirdi and decided to spend some time there, and seek Sai's guidance, for, while reading the *Jnaneshwari*, doubts and misapprehensions would arise in his mind, and he would not be able to digest what he read. So he came to Shirdi, and resolved that when Sai himself would inspire him with love and tell him to read, only then would he make a beginning, with no doubts in his mind.

Jog met Deo, and asked him, "Why do you not read the *Jnaneshwari* regularly these days?" When Deo said that he would commence only when Baba told him to read, Jog said, "Bring the book and place it in Baba's hands. When he returns it to you, then you can start reading it."

But Deo did not approve of this, for Baba knew his mind and there was no need for this ruse. Then he took *darshan* of Baba, and offered one rupee at his feet.

"Why only one? Bring twenty," said Baba to him.

So he gave him the desired money. At night he met Balakram, and asked him how he had won Baba's grace. Balakram said that he would tell him everything the following day after *arati*.

The following day, when Deo went to the mosque for Baba's *darshan*, Baba asked him for twenty rupees which he gave very gladly. Since the mosque was very crowded, he stood aside.

Baba asked, "Where is he hidden in some awkward place in all this crowd?"

Deo replied, "Here I am Baba." Baba asked him why he had given him only seven rupees, and Deo corrected him by saying that he had given him twenty rupees.

"Whose money is it?" Baba asked.

"Baba, it is yours."

"Then why are you running away? Come and sit near me, with your mind at ease."

Deo faithfully obeyed Sai's command. The *arati* was performed, and everyone went home, Deo returning with Balakram. He again asked him the same question, and Balakram told him what had happened. Deo then said to him, "Did he tell you how to meditate on the Brahman? Do satisfy my desire for knowledge!" And as Balakram was about to answer, Chandru appeared, and said that Baba wanted to see Deo. Without a moment's delay, Deo came to meet Sai.

Deo at once made obeisance to Sai, who then asked him with whom he had been conversing. Deo replied that he had been listening to Sai's glory from Balakram. Baba said, "Bring twenty five rupees," which Deo immediately brought and offered to Baba.

"How many have you brought?" Baba enquired. When Deo said that he had brought twenty five rupees, Baba told him to come and sit with him in the mosque. Baba sat near the pillar, and there was no one else in the mosque. Baba said, "You have stolen my piece of rag without my knowledge."

Deo said that he knew of no rag. Then Baba said, "Then it must be somewhere here only. You search for it. This tendency of yours is evil. Maybe some mischievous child has taken it! See, it must be here somewhere." Deo searched but could not find it.

Looking around hither and thither, Sai wrinkled his brows, glared at Deo, and roared at him as if in rage,

"You are yourself a cheat! Who else except you will come at this time to steal a piece of rag? I consider you to be the thief. Have you come here to steal? Though you have aged, you haven't yet got rid of your bad habit! I will strike you with an axe! I will cut you up, kill you! Where can you escape from my hands? Wherever you go, I will kill you there! You come to Shirdi all the way to steal? Take back your money, and return my piece of rag!"

Sai ranted and raved, indulging in abuses in the wildest terms, his face flushed with fury. Deo gazed at him with awe and admiration, realising that he was alone with Sai, and that he might be in for some beating too. Maybe Baba was revealing the spectacular vision of the Cosmic Form, and this thought filled him with sheer joy. Yet, he also wondered about the rag which seemed to have put Baba in such a temper.

Baba said, "Go, get out of here!" and Deo moved towards the steps. After about twelve minutes, he again stood before Baba who promptly showered abuses on him. "Why have you come again? Go away, be gone to the *wada!*" Baba ordered. Deo obeyed respectfully, and making obeisance at Baba's feet, returned to the *wada.* He narrated to Balakram and Jog all that had happened at the mosque. For twenty four minutes Baba abused and cursed loudly. Then after four or five hours, he began to call people to him.

Deo also went and sat with the others at the

mosque. Sai said, "The old man must have been hurt by the abuses that I rained on him. But he had stolen the piece of rag. Then what could be done? I could not help saying it! But Allah will see everything. He too will bless him."

Then, that compassionate and ever-forgiving Sai said, "Bhau, will you give *dakshina*?"

"How much shall I bring?" asked Deo.

"Bring twelve quickly," said Baba.

But when he looked into his pocket, he found that he had a single note, and he told Baba so. Baba then said, "Let it be, I do not want it. In the morning you gave me twice. I did not remember it." But Deo obtained the required amount and handed it over to Baba, making obeisance at his feet.

Baba asked Deo, "What do you do these days?" and Deo said that he had nothing much to do.

Baba suggested, "Go on reading the *pothi* regularly. You should sit in the *wada* and read the *pothi* every day, and at the same time, give an exposition faithfully each day to all. When I sit here ready to give you a whole shawl, resplendent with *zari* work, why do you have to steal pieces of rags? Why do you indulge in this piece of stealing?"

So Deo started reading the *Jnaneshwari* regularly thenceforth, while also giving an exposition. His wish was fulfilled by Baba's permission, and the anxiety in his heart laid to rest. He gradually understood the significance of the pieces of rags and shawl with *zari* work—instead of asking Baba about how to meditate on the Brahman, how to be guided to the *upasana*, etc., he had approached Balakram for enlightenment. This had sent Baba into a rage, for was he not the Divine Instructor who was a virtual store of divine knowledge? Then why seek some other mortal for guidance? Was he not always there ready to answer any questions or clarify all doubts?

Although outwardly Sai appeared to be angry, in his heart he was full of compassion and love for his devotees. Deo's heart was overwhelmed with a deep love and gratitude for Baba. One Thursday in April 1914, at dawn, he received the grace of Baba in a dream. He asked Deo, "Do you understand the *pothi*?" When Deo shook his head, he again asked, "When is it going to be understood?" Deo's eyes filled with tears, and he said, "Unless I receive your grace, reading the *pothi* is a futile exercise. It is even more difficult to understand it, and I confess to you frankly."

Baba said, "While reading the *pothi*, you do so hastily. Now sit near me and read it loudly. Read first the chapter on spiritual matters." Deo rose to fetch the book, and he woke up from his dream. So Deo got instructions from the right source even in his dream, such is the *leela* of Sai Samarth.

How wonderful are Baba's *leelas* and how

effortlessly they come about! Shama, a very trusted and loyal devotee of Baba was always amazed by them. Once, Kakasaheb Dikshit decided to celebrate the thread ceremony of his eldest son at Nagpur. Around the same time, Nanasaheb Chandorkar's son was also getting married at Gwalior. Nana decided that it would not be possible for Kaka to attend his son's wedding as the dates clashed, so he postponed it to a slightly later date, to facilitate Kaka's attending the wedding. He went to Shirdi, and making obeisance to Baba, invited him to attend his son's wedding. Baba said, "All right," then said, "take Shama with you." Two days later, Kaka too extended his invitation to Baba to attend his son's thread ceremony. To him too Baba said, "Take Shama with you." Kaka pressed Baba to be present there himself, and Baba said, "After visiting Kashi-Prayag quickly, I will arrive even before Shama. What can delay my coming there?"

Shama (alias Madhavrao) thought, 'Once I go to Gwalior, Kashi is not far from there!' He borrowed money from Nandaram for his expenses, and went to Baba to take his permission. He asked him most respectfully, "Now that I am going up to Nagpur, then to Gwalior, I think it only proper that Kashi-Prayag should also be visited. Hence, O God, I bow at your feet and pray, shall I visit Kashi-Gaya also?"

Baba consented with pleasure, and said, "What is improper in what you ask? Whatever comes about easily, effortlessly, should most certainly and without fail be availed of."

Shama set off for Kopergaon in a bullock cart, and there he met Appa Kote. When the latter heard of Shama's proposal to visit Kashi, he too was tempted to join the holy company of Shama for such a pilgrimage. Though he lacked funds right then, Shama assured him that he would take him. So they first attended the thread ceremony at Nagpur where Kakasaheb gave two hundred rupees to Nana for his expenses.

They then went to Gwalior where Nana presented a hundred rupees to Shama, and the bride's father gave him a hundred rupees as well. After visiting Mathura, they went to Prayag, and then to Ayodhya just in time for the Ramanavami celebrations. They spent twenty one days there, and two months at Kashi. After the sun and moon eclipses, they set out for Gaya.

On reaching Gaya, they discovered that plague had broken out there. In great fear Shama and Kote halted in a rest house for the night. In the morning, a Brahmin came for them and said, "Come on, hurry up! The whole crowd of pilgrims has set out to go." When Shama voiced his fears, the Brahmin assured them that his place was free of any such epidemic. So they went to his place, and were glad to see his spacious house.

As they sat down, Shama was overwhelmed with joy on seeing Baba's picture right in front of him. They had never even imagined that Baba's picture would adorn someone's house so far away from Shirdi. His eyes filled with tears of love and joy, and the Brahmin, mistaking them for tears of fear and apprehension, consoled them by saying, "I have already told you that here there is no plague, and yet you worry. I am really surprised! If you have no faith in me, then ask the others." But Shama was only remembering Baba's words: "Visiting Kashi-Prayag quickly, I will arrive even before Shama," and was experiencing the truth of the words.

Shama asked the Brahmin how he had secured Baba's picture, and the latter narrated the incident thus. He had two to three hundred people on his payroll, and he used to maintain a full, detailed register of pilgrims at Manmad and Puntambe. He had to make necessary arrangements for the pilgrims, and his work once took him to Shirdi. He had heard a lot about the greatness of Sai Samarth, and he wished to have his *darshan*. So he went to the mosque, and making his obeisance at Baba's feet, he had a good *darshan* of him. As he felt a keen desire to have Baba's picture, he asked Shama for the one which was hanging on the wall. With Baba's permission he gave him the picture, and this is how he happened to have Sai's picture in his house.

Shama then remembered the incident, and realised that this was the same picture of Baba and the same Brahmin who had taken it from him. Inscrutable are Baba's ways and *leelas*, for he had sent Shama to the same Brahmin who had visited him twelve years earlier, and had also given his *darshan* with this picture. The

Brahmin too recollected that Shama was the same person who had handed over the picture to him. Their joy knew no bounds, and Shama was treated royally, and his pilgrimage was completed satisfactorily due to Baba's grace.

Baba's love for his devotees was indeed very deep, and he always saved them in distress through his *leelas*. One day as Baba went for a walk in the morning after his usual repast, he reached the bank of a river, and stayed there to rest a while. He washed his feet, then took a bath, feeling refreshed. He sat down leisurely in the shade of a cluster of trees. Since he wanted to fill his clay pipe, he went to the river again to wet the piece of rag that he used to wrap around the pipe. Just then he heard a croaking sound, one similar to that of a frog.

He returned to the shade, and with the flint, lit the clay pipe, soon ready for smoking. Suddenly a wayfarer appeared before him, and making obeisance to Baba, sat near him. With great humility he invited Baba to his house nearby, saying that Baba had come very far, and it would be too hot for him to return to his abode soon. He said he would give him something to eat, and he could rest a while.

The frog again was heard to be croaking loudly and piteously. So the wayfarer asked, "Who is this crying aloud?"

Baba said, "A frog is in trouble near the river bank. His *karma* is pursuing him. Listen to the story that I shall narrate to you." The wayfarer wanted to be sure that it was a frog and not some other creature crying. So Baba said, "Go and see for yourself how the frog, fallen in the jaws of a big snake, is crying out. Both, in fact, are wicked. They had sinned terribly in the past birth, and to pay for them, they have these bodies in this birth."

The wayfarer returned, confirming Baba's words, saying, "What you say is true. That snake has a monstrous jaw, and the frog too is frightened. The frog will last only for a short while".

Baba said, "How can he put that frog to rest? Am I, his Father, not sitting here? What am I needed for? Now that I have come, just watch how I release him! Let us see what the snake does next!"

The wayfarer filled the pipe again, and lighting it, puffed it once and then presented it to Baba. Baba puffed at it twice, and then proceeded with him to the site where the snake and frog were battling with life. The wayfarer warned Baba not to go near as he feared the snake would attack them. But just then Baba said, "Oh Veerabhadrappa, has not this Basappa, your enemy, yet repented, even after being born a frog. And you too are born a snake, yet such mortal enmity? Oh, have some shame, at least now! Give up the enmity and be at peace!"

No sooner had Baba finished speaking than the snake released the frog and slid away quickly out of sight. The frog too disappeared into the vegetation. The wayfarer could hardly believe his eyes! He said, "I do not understand this at all! Oh, the moment your words came out, the snake released the frog and quickly disappeared! Who are this Veerabhadrappa and Basappa? Oh, please tell me!"

Baba took him to the shade of the trees, and smoking the pipe, related the past events. Just six miles beyond where Baba lived was an old, famous, holy land on which stood an ancient, dilapidated temple of Mahadev (Shiva). The people collected a big subscription with the intention of renovating it. A wealthy man of that place was in charge of administering the renovation, and had custody of the money collected. He had to maintain separate accounts and add to the funds his own subscription amount in cash. Since he was a miser, his wealth remained with him, and the temple work was progressing ever so slowly.

When all the money was exhausted, and the renovation work still incomplete, he still had no heart to spend anything from his pocket, in spite of being such a wealthy man. He was also a money lender, and greed was second nature to him.

People were helpless. They collected more money, and handing it over to him, they entreated him to get the job completed, but it was a futile effort. He did nothing, and the work was left pending. His wife had a vision in which she was told, "You, at least, wake up and build a dome to the temple. Mahadev will give you a hundredfold of what you spend." When she narrated this to her husband, he would have nothing of it, for how could he spend so much money which fetched no returns? He ridiculed her by saying that God could have approached him directly in his dream. What was the necessity of appearing in her dream? Therefore he was not convinced, nor could he understand the significance. Either the dream was false, or else it was a divine effort to split their marriage. He was trying his best to complete the renovation, but the money that they had all put in was also being depleted quickly. It was a great loss to him to handle this commercial system of accounts, and people failed to see this. He told her that this vision was probably the effect of a disturbed sleep, and left it at that.

The wife fell silent. But then she had another dream in which God told her to give whatever little she wished to give, as even one coin, sincerely given, was like a lakh of rupees. He told her to consult her husband, and give whatever little she could spare, only devotion and faith mattered. He who gave without a loving faith, his offering would have no value and would be utterly fruitless. So she resolved to sell the ornaments given to her by her father during her marriage, to meet this demand.

When she told this to her husband, his mind was greatly disturbed. He decided to have all her ornaments valued, and a piece of land transferred to her name instead. So he bought all her ornaments, and instead of money, gave her a piece of land, which was a waste land on which nothing grew. So he said to his wife to offer the land to Lord Shankara, and He would be pleased with this offer. So she lovingly offered what she had to her Lord Shankara.

This land had belonged to Dubaki, a poor woman who had mortgaged it to this money lender against a loan of two hundred rupees. The money lender was avaricious, always greedy for more and more wealth. Such pursuit of sensual pleasures only brings destruction. What he had asked his wife to offer Lord Shankara was devoid of any merit, and he paid the price for it.

One day, a raging storm struck the village, during which all constructions were razed to the ground by lightning. The only thing that was left was the land. Most of the people died, including the money lender, his wife, and Dubaki.

Later, the money lender was born to a poor Brahmin in Mathura, his wife to a priest, and Dubaki as a male child to one who worked in the temple and was a Shiva devotee. While the moneylender was called Veerabhadra, his wife was Gauri, and Dubaki born as a boy was Chanabasappa.

Gauri grew up to be a fine girl, while the priest became a fond companion of Baba. Gauri also used to come with her father, and worship Baba. One day the priest said that he was tired of looking out for a suitable groom for his daughter. Baba assured him that the groom was already on the way, so why worry? He would come to the priest's house and accept his daughter's hand in marriage.

Veerabhadra, being subjected to utter poverty, set out from his house, assuring his parents that he would earn some money. He went from village to village, sometimes begging for alms, at other times earning by manual labour. As he wandered he arrived at the priest's house. Everyone in the area liked him.

Gradually, the priest too became impressed by him. One day he took him to see Baba, who, pleased with him, said, "If an auspicious day can be fixed for the wedding, give Gauri to him and be free of the responsibility."

Soon a suitable day was chosen for the wedding, and the couple were married in a most fitting manner. They came for Baba's *darshan* and blessings, and Veerabhadra started enjoying the comfort, happiness and square meals. He soon started worshipping Baba. Then he set up his home, and shortly he began to feel the pinch of money. He went to Baba and said, "Baba, these marriage bonds have left me drained of money. Please show me some way out so that I can cope with these family burdens. I fall at your feet in supplication and humility. Please help me!"

Baba assured him that he would soon have enough and more, and he need not worry any more. But Veerabhadra said that he scorned wealth, but he was tired of his wife's endless demands, and married life was becoming sour for him.

Then an amazing thing took place, all being Baba's *leela.* That land which belonged to Gauri, and was lying vacant, shot up in value. A buyer approached them and bought the land for one lakh rupees, paying half in cash on the spot, and promising to pay the remaining in instalments of two thousand per year over the next twenty five years.

Everyone was delighted, but Chanabasappa objected, saying, that since he worked in the temple, he was entitled to be the first owner of the money that was offered to Shiva. He said half the yearly interest was for him as his share. Veerabhadra and Chanabasappa thus got into a heated argument, and they came to Baba. The great saint told them that Shankara was the absolute master of the land which could not be of any use to anyone else, and so not to get enmeshed in greed. Only Gauri could use it, anyone else desiring it would starve to death, bringing the wrath of God upon himself. Even Veerabhadra could not act independently on his own, without Gauri's consent.

As Veerabhadra heard this advice from Baba, he was very angry with Baba and showered abuses on him, saying that Baba himself planned to usurp the lot. He raved and ranted against his wife at home, and she went to Baba and entreated him not to be displeased with her after hearing the abuses from her husband, but have a kind thought for her, his daughter. Baba assured her that his grace would always be with her.

That night Shiva appeared in her dream and instructed her not to give the money to anyone as it was all hers. She was to follow Chanabasappa's instructions on how to expend it for the temple, for He trusted him. If the money had to be spent on other works, Baba in the mosque should be first consulted, to prevent any mismanagement of the funds.

When she narrated this dream to Baba, he advised her to follow it as ordained, giving half the interest from the capital to Chanabasappa, and that Veerabhadra had no concern in this matter.

Just then Veerabhadra and Chanabasappa arrived there, arguing senselessly and heatedly. When Baba explained to them about Lord Shiva's instructions to Gauri in her dream, Veerabhadra was furious. He abused them volubly, raving and ranting deliriously, then said to Chanabasappa, "Whenever I catch you, I will destroy you! I will cut you up into pieces and then swallow them all up!"

Chanabasappa, scared out of his wits, fell at Baba's feet, and clinging to them tightly, begged him to free him from this calamity. Baba assured him of his protection, and of not letting him die at the hands of Veerabhadra.

Later on, Veerabhadra had gone into a delirium and died. He was reborn as a snake. Chanabasappa, always in mortal dread, died soon after, and was born as a frog. As events unfolded later, Veerabhadra held him in the jaws of death, and hearing Basappa's piteous cries, Baba liberated him from the clutches of Veerabhadra, in the form of the snake.

What divine *leela* indeed! An endless saga of fascinating *leelas* that continue to captivate devotees' hearts even today, for these *leelas* have not stopped happening, they still continue to be performed by Sadguru Sai, even today.

5

Sai's Bestowal of Grace

Whenever Baba was ever willing and ready to favour the devotee with his grace, it behove and became the sacred duty of the devotee to become receptive to receive such grace. He could become such a fortunate one by leading a chaste, pure, simple and virtuous life. By repenting and confessing his sins to Baba, his guilt would be washed away by Sai's grace. He could then trustfully and sincerely look up to Baba to lead him on the righteous and virtuous path, and raise him to a higher and higher plane till he merged with the One.

Bestowal of grace on one depended on one's earnestness and intensity of devotion. Baba might grace one by arousing one's spiritual awakening by a touch or otherwise. His methods of bestowing grace varied from person to person depending upon his merit. Blessed are those devotees who, by rare good fortune, are enriched in his saintly company!

Tatya and Mahlsapati were indeed very fortunate! They both had the privilege of Baba's company equally. They both slept with Baba in the mosque. The love that Baba had for them was something spectacular and unique. They used to lie down with their feet in the centre of the room, their heads in different directions east, west and north. Their feet would touch each other's at the centre. Lying on their sheets, they would keep on talking on all matters. If one of them dozed or appeared to be dozing, another would wake him up.

If Tatya started snoring, Baba would suddenly get up, and turning him upside down, would press his head down. With Mahlsapati's help, he would clasp Tatya closely, squeeze him tight, press his leg and rub his back vigorously. In this way, Tatya slept with Baba for fourteen years in the mosque. He had left his parents to be with Baba always, out of great fondness for him. Who can measure or assess the value of Baba's grace?

Once Tatya wanted to go to Kopergaon to attend the weekly market. He came to Baba to take his permission, and bowed at his feet. The *tonga* was waiting outside and Tatya was impatient to go. But Baba said to him, "Just wait a moment! The marketing can be done later, do not go outside the village now."

But Tatya was impatient and insistent, so Baba said, "Do take Shama with you." Tatya thought there was no need for anyone to accompany him, and so he disregarded Baba's advice. He had hired the swifter of the two *tongas*, and soon he was on his way to Kopergaon.

As he approached a small village, the horse began

to gallop very fast, becoming wild and uncontrollable. Shortly thereafter, it tripped and fell, giving a sudden, violent jolt to the *tonga*, and spraining Tatya's loins sorely. He immediately remembered Sai's words and regretted not having heeded his advice. But nothing could be done at that time, and he realised his foolishness.

At another time, Tatya set out to go to Kolhar, and he had the horses harnessed to a *tonga*. Then he went to Baba, and bowing at his feet, said, "I will be back in no time." Although Baba had not said a word or given his consent, Tatya set out. The horses were wild, and ran unbridled, while the *tonga* was light and small. The horses ran pell-mell over ditches and pits, and Tatya's life stood in great danger. But Sai's grace saved him, for the *tonga* hit a tree, and broke down. Thus Baba saved him from further disasters. Sai's grace is the fruit of our penance of several births. It gives us a joy as boundless as that of a thirsty wayfarer who finds drinking water in a desert.

A well-known gentleman named Sathe during Lord Ray's tenure as governor of Bombay Presidency, became an ardent devotee of Sai Baba. How he came to be blessed by Baba's grace is indeed wondrous. He had suffered a great loss in business, and soon felt weary and disgusted with the worldly life. Greatly agitated in mind, he decided to go to a place where there was absolute solitude. During such a time, he remembered God and called out to Him frantically.

Some of his friends suggested that he go to Shirdi for Sainath's *darshan* and pray to the most compassionate saint. Even a moment in his august company would steady and calm his agitated mind. This advice sounded like nectar to his ears, and he at once resolved to visit Shirdi.

He arrived at the village, took the *darshan* of Sai Baba, and prostrated at his feet. He was full of calm and peace within, and his heart was full of joy. As a man of great determination, he started reading the *Guru Charitra* regularly and with great perseverance.

On the seventh night when he completed reading the book, Baba appeared with a book in his hand, and began to explain to Sathe the meaning of the book *Guru Charitra*. While Baba sat with the book in his hand, expounding its meaning, Sathe sat listening calmly and respectfully to the exposition. His heart was filled with love for Baba, and he thanked Baba from awakening him from a sleep of ignorance by feeding him the *Guru Charitra*. He woke up soon after.

He narrated this dream to Kakasaheb in great detail, and said he failed to understand the underlying message in this dream. Only Baba could explain it, and would Kaka, please, ask him about it. Since he had read it, did it mean that Baba wished him to begin another reading of the book?

When Kaka approached Baba with this question, Baba told him that Sathe should read it once more, for by reading this sacred story of the guru, devotees became pure, God would be pleased, and they would be freed from the bondage of worldly life.

While Baba was explaining thus to Kaka, Hemadpant was sitting beside Baba and pressing his legs. He thought that Sathe had read the sacred book for just a week, and he was enjoying its just reward, while he, Hemadpant, had been reading it for forty years, and Baba had not satisfied his ardent wish.

This thought was immediately discerned by Baba. Out of such ignorance, thousands and thousands of desires arise instantly in the mind, but Baba knows all these desires. Baba, however, overlooks all that is objectionable, and encourages and motivates at the right time all the good and generous actions.

Reading Hemadpant's thoughts, Baba said to him, "Get up, go to Shama and fetch fifteen rupees. Sit and converse with him for a while, and then return with the *dakshina* that he gives."

Hemadpant went to Shama's place just as Shama, after his bath, was arranging his *dhoti*, murmuring *naam*. Seeing his friend, Shama asked him how was it that he had come alone, at this hour, from the mosque. He looked worried too. Shama asked Hemadpant to be seated while he finished his *puja*, then they could talk.

Hemadpant idly picked up a copy of *Nath Bhagvat*, and opened it at random. To his amazement it was the same page that he had left incomplete in the morning. Since he had neglected to complete it, Baba had sent him here with this purpose, thereby disciplining him. He realised that he should not have quit reading the book till he had completed it. He had read half of a story, and as everybody was setting out for the mosque, he too had rushed with them, thus neglecting his daily routine of reading it.

When Shama joined him after completing his *puja*, Hemadpant told him the purpose of his visit. Shama was surprised to hear about wanting fifteen rupees as *dakshina* from him. So he said that instead of rupees, give Baba his respectful salutations as his *dakshina*. Then Hemadpant asked him to relate stories of Baba as listening to them would wash away all his sins.

Shama said, "Inscrutable are Sai Baba's *leelas*. I am but an uneducated rustic, and you are all city-dwellers. To you, what can I say of his incomprehensible *leelas?*" He then went on to say that no one can understand his *leelas* and skilful ways. His sport is endless, and while he plays the game, he is never in it. All the ardent seekers of knowledge are learned, one more than another, so how can ignorant villagers understand Baba's inconceivable life? Instead of telling his story himself, why had Baba sent him to Shama? He alone knows his ways, which are not human, but divine.

Then Shama said that he was reminded of a nice story, an incident which took place in Shirdi before his very eyes. This would show that whatover be one's resolve, Baba would see to its proper fulfilment.

Sometimes Baba put one to a severe test to test one's love and devotion, and only then gave one his spiritual instruction.

The moment Hemadpant heard the words 'spiritual instruction', he remembered at once the incident of Sathe's *Guru Charitra* like a flash of lightning. Could this be Baba's way of steadying his agitated mind? Strange were Baba's ways! Then, as he listened to the stories of Baba's *leelas*, his compassion for the devotees, his style of functioning, etc., he felt elated and joyous.

Shama related to him the story of Radhabai Deshmukh, who suddenly decided to spend all her time in the holy company of saints. Having heard about the greatness of Sai Baba, she came to Shirdi with others from Sanganer. She took his *darshan* with humility and great respect, an answering faith in him deeply embedded in her heart. Seeing him, all the exhaustion of her travel left her, filling her with great joy and peace. She wanted to make him her guru, so that she could make her spiritual progress under his divine guidance.

But she had one resolution, that until he gave her some *mantra* in her ear, and thus made her worthy of his grace, she would not leave Shirdi. Having made this firm resolution in her mind, she gave up all food and drink. At such an old age, she refused to take even a sip of water, such was her steadfast faith and trust in Baba.

She continued to fast thus for three days, determined to carry her vow to its very end, come what may! At the end of the third day, she became exhausted and dejected.

Shama was worried by her state of health, for the dauntless lady was not afraid of death. So he went to the mosque, and seated himself in front of Baba. Baba asked him, as usual, about the well-being of all, and then said that the oil man, Narayan, had gone astray, and was troubling him unnecessarily.

Shama said to Baba, "What is this mystery of yours, Oh God? No one can understand your ways. You bring people, one by one, to this village and ask us for news! That Radhabai, old and obstinate that she is, has remained without food and water to win your grace. Her faith in you is unshakable, though she is very adamant. And you—you do not even look at her! Why do you make her so unhappy? Soon her life will ebb away, and people will say that she wanted spiritual instruction from you, but you let her die, which will be most improper. Really, I see no hope for her! Do tell her something yourself!"

Seeing the determination of the old lady, Baba called out to her affectionately, and said, "Mother, why do you sit so adamantly, observing a fast? Why do you think of giving up your life thus?" His words were very soothing and melodious to her ears. He made her sit before him, and passed on lovingly to her the secret of his greatness thus, "Mother, tell me truly, why do you inflict so much suffering on yourself? I am but a *fakir* who goes around begging for alms. Be kind to me! Really, I am your son, and you, my father." Then he told her a wonderful story which, he said, would give her great happiness.

Baba's guru was a great saint, full of compassion. Baba went on serving his guru till he was exhausted, but his guru would not whisper the *mantra* in his ear. Baba too, like the lady, was determined not to give up his efforts in receiving the guru *mantra*. In the beginning, his guru tricked him by asking from him only two pice. When this was paid, the *mantra* was still not forthcoming. Baba had doubts—his guru had no desires, then why did he ask for money? How could he then be free from desires? No, what did his guru want with money, for that was not his idea. Baba then realised what the two pice stood for—faith and forbearance, and nothing else. Baba gave these immediately to his guru who then was very pleased with his disciple.

So for twelve years Baba served his guru with forbearance and unswerving faith, a guru who was the image of devotion and pure love. There was no scarcity of food or clothes, nor of love and affection. Baba's joy in his guru's company was pure and unlimited. As he looked at his guru's face, Baba's eyes would be absorbed in meditation, giving both teacher-disciple an experience of bliss. Day and night Baba gazed into his face, knowing no hunger, no thirst. His guru was the only objective, the constant goal.

The guru too expected only this, and nothing beyond this. He never treated Baba with indifference or unconcern, and always protected him in his troubles. Sometimes Baba would remain at his feet, and always had the joy of his company, while his guru would wash him with loving glances.

Then Baba said to Radhabai, "Mother, accept it as the truth what I tell you, sitting in the mosque. If the guru never whispered the *mantra* even in my ears, how can I whisper it in yours? I really know no other instruction. So I say, why persist in the futile efforts for a *mantra*? Now go and eat some food, do not put your life in danger. Only have steadfast faith in me, and your spiritual progress will grow. You look up to me with single-minded devotion, and I will look after you similarly. My guru never taught me anything else."

The old lady was deeply moved, and placing her hand on Baba's feet, she ended her vow.

When Shama finished reciting this tale of Baba and Radhabai Deshmukh, Hemadpant could hardly contain the great joy within, and his throat choked with emotion. This excellent lesson was deeply ingrained in his mind.

Shama asked him why he had become so silent all of a sudden. There were so many such stories. Just then the bell at the mosque was heard. So they both went to the mosque. The *arati* was in progress, and the steps leading into the mosque jam-packed. Hemadpant decided to remain outside till the *arati* was over, then go to Baba for his *darshan*. But Shama pulled him up the steps and took him straight to Baba.

Baba was seated in his usual place, while Jog was performing the *arati*, with the bell tinkling in his left hand. Shama sat before Baba and made Hemadpant sit at the right of Baba, facing Baba. Then Baba demanded from Hemadpant the *dakshina* that Shama had given to him. Hemadpant said that Shama, who was also there, had given salutations instead of fifteen rupees. Then Baba asked him to narrate all that had been spoken between him and Shama.

Hemadpant eagerly told Baba all that they had talked about which had delighted his heart. The story about the old lady had indeed been marvellous. As Shama had told him the story, Hemadpant had realised that Baba's ways were inconceivable. It was as if Baba had most certainly conferred his grace on him, under the pretext of the story. Baba told him to narrate the story so that he too could see what was so wonderful about it.

Hemadpant had heard it just some time ago, so without faltering, he narrated it to Baba, who was pleased to listen to it. Then Baba said, "Keep this carefully in mind. How sweet is the story you have just heard! Have you really found it meaningful?"

Hemadpant replied, "Baba, after listening to this story, I felt at peace with myself. The doubts and worries in my mind have disappeared, and I have found a definite path."

Baba told him to maintain the oneness between the guru and the disciple, be free from all desires, and meditate on Supreme Pure Consciousness that is Blissful Joy.

Just then the *arati* rituals concluded, and Jog offered lump-sugar to Baba who put out his palm to receive it. This he emptied into Hemadpant's hand, and said, "If you bear this well in mind, your condition will be as this sugar-candy. Just as this is sweet, similarly, the wishes of your heart will be fulfilled, and you will be blessed with good fortune."

Hemadpant made obeisance to Baba, praying for his divine grace, and said, "This alone is enough for me! Please be with me!"

Baba advised him to constantly remember the story, "meditate upon it repeatedly, and joy will manifest itself. That which you have heard, store in your heart, and your sins will be washed away."

Another tale involving Hemadpant shows how Baba strengthens one's good resolves, encourages good deeds, and confers his grace without even being asked for it. One night, as he lay in bed, his mind was focused on Shri Rama till he fell asleep. As he woke up in the morning, *Rama-naam* came to his mind, and he started chanting it.

With thoughts of Rama preoccupying his mind, he set out for the mosque to have the morning *darshan* o

Baba, taking with him whatever flowers he could lay his hands on. Just as he neared Buty-wada, he heard Aurangabadkar, one of Baba's devotees, singing a hymn in praise of Lord Rama. Hearing it, his joy knew no bounds! He realised at once that the compassionate Baba had read his innermost thoughts, and this was one of his ways of giving him a direct and definite experience. Without uttering a word, he unmistakably gave in his hands the best form of worship. Baba needed no particular place or time to instruct his devotees.

Another story that follows brings out Sai's kindness and all-pervasiveness, while conferring his grace on the devotee. A certain devotee was once lured into entertaining uncharitable thoughts, and soon he started criticising everybody and everything. The listeners were disgusted with such behaviour from him. They ignored him and went towards the mosque for Baba's *darshan*, while the critic went towards the stream for his morning ablutions.

Baba had a clearly intuitive knowledge of all that was going on. He was returning with his devotees from Lendi Bagh when he enquired about the critic. When they replied that he had gone for his morning ablutions, Baba turned his steps towards the mosque. Soon he met the critic returning from the stream. Baba pointed out to the devotees a village sow that was feasting on excrement near a compound fence, and said, "See, how that tongue relishes crushing and mashing the excrement of the public, to gratify her inordinate desire for venting her anger on her kith and kin. He who fritters away this precious human birth which has come to him as a result of great past merit and is thus bent on self-destruction, to such a one, what happiness or peace can this Shirdi give?"

Baba went on speaking thus, and the critic realised that these words of Baba were directed towards him for his own benefit. He recollected the happenings of the morning, when he had criticised everyone, and he felt ashamed of his behaviour. When the significance of his precious words is carefully retained in the heart, can spiritual advancement be far behind?

Once a well-known saint named Pir Maulana in Bombay drew a lot of people to him from various parts of India. Hemadpant was a magistrate in the suburb at that time, and Maulana's devotee, Yunus, persuaded him to go for the Maulana's *darshan*. Though thousands of people flocked to see him, Hemadpant was reluctant for he did not like to be persuaded, and he found other excuses not to have his *darshan*.

After many years passed, he was transferred from there. But later on, when the right time came, he had the good fortune to have a lasting association with Baba. Nevertheless, when the proper time comes and the occasion demands, these saints incarnate at the place of their choice to accomplish their purpose. They each know the mind of the other thoroughly, for at heart, they are all one. Similarly, Baba appears in different places, and steers his ship of devotees smoothly by guiding its course secretly.

Once a gentleman, well educated, gradually rose to be a renowned officer. Later, he became a *mamlatdar*, a rank similar to that of a Deputy Collector. Though the post was once considered to be high and prestigious, in the later days, it only meant more responsibilities and headaches. In Vadgaon, near Belgaum, a contingent of surveyors came on a visit and camped there. He too went there, and had the *darshan* of a saintly man, who said to him, with a book named *Vicharsagar* in his hand, "So, you may go now. But have a look at this book. Remember that by doing so, your wishes will be fulfilled. And later, as you proceed northwards, you will have the good fortune of the *darshan* of a great saint. This great person will guide you in life, bringing stability and peace of mind. He will himself then instruct you, and imprint his teachings on your mind."

He was soon transferred to Junnar, and to reach it he had to cross over Naneghat which would prove to be perilous for crossing owing to its great height. So he procured a buffalo as the mode of transport. Having saddled it with stuffed cushions, he mounted the buffalo and set out. The journey was quite arduous and backbreaking, but at last he reached Junnar.

Then, after some time, he was transferred to Kalyan where he met Nanasaheb Chandorkar. On hearing about the greatness of Sainath, he too wished to have his *darshan*. So they decided to leave for Shirdi the following day to have Baba's *darshan*, and after spending a day or two there, they would return to Kalyan.

But on the day of the journey, he had to forsake going to Shirdi with Nana, as the hearing of a case had come up in the Thane Civil Court. Nana urged him not to abandon the visit, for Baba was all-powerful, and would satisfy his desire for his *darshan*. In comparison to this, the court case was of less importance. But he was not convinced, and was afraid of missing the hearing, so he went to Thane.

To his great amazement, the matter got adjourned to a future date. Now he felt let down, for the court matter was postponed, and he had missed Baba's *darshan* also. But he immediately set out for Shirdi. Probably Nana would still be there and guide him to Baba. The place would be new and he knew no one there.

In the meanwhile, Nana had gone to the mosque for Baba's *darshan*, and had started on his return journey. When the gentleman reached Shirdi, he, of course, could not find Nana, but fortunately, he met someone he knew and so could be taken to Baba.

On having Baba's *darshan*, the gentleman prostrated in obeisance before Sai. He was filled with joy, love and adoration, his eyes brimming over with overwhelming emotion. Then as he stood up to take his leave, Baba said, "What the saint told you was like climbing the *ghat* mounted on a buffalo. But it is not so easy to tread on this path. Here it is inevitable that one wears out one's body in hard toil".

As these words were significant, his heart overflowed with greater happiness. What the saint at Vadgaon had said was true. With folded hands, he placed his head on Sai's feet, and said, "Maharaj, have mercy on me, take me under your wing. You alone are my guru. Only today I have understood the underlying message of the book *Vicharsagar*, and thus experienced the highest pleasure. Oh, where is that Vadgaon, and where is Shirdi! And what a pair indeed, of the saint and the saintly!" He told Baba how the saint had predicted that he would meet Baba who would steer his course of life, and that he should read the book, which he had done.

Baba then replied, "What Appa told you was perfectly right! But when you put all that into practice, only then will your wishes be fulfilled." And so the gentleman, with the grace and blessings of Sai, followed his advice to rise to a higher level of consciousness.

Baba's intuitive knowledge was indeed so unique, that people were always amazed by him. Once a lawyer came to the mosque for Baba's *darshan*. He bowed at his feet, then offered the *dakshina* that he carried with him, and sat down beside him. Then he watched and listened to Baba's conversation with the others.

Baba suddenly turned towards him and said, "Oh,

how insincere people are! They will bow at the feet, even offer *dakshina,* and yet curse you all the time in their heart! How strange, indeed!"

The lawyer immediately realised that Baba's words were meant for him, and he felt thoroughly ashamed of himself for he was guilty. He bowed his head in shame and kept quiet. Later, he met Dikshit at the *wada,* and told him that what Baba had said was absolutely right. He had been with the *munsif* (civil judge) and other lawyers in the common room when the *munsif* retired to his home due to ill-health. Taking about him, one of them said, "Can these physical ailments be cured, in the absence of proper medication, merely by going after Sai? Does it behove such a man as the *munsif* to behave thus?" Even discussions about Sai were in a negative vein. Even this lawyer was party to such discussions, and Baba, being omniscient, knew all that had transpired there, and hence the verbal attack on him, which he richly deserved. This was yet one more proof that though a hundred miles away, Sai knew everybody's mind. He was truly omniscient and omnipresent. From then onwards, the lawyer firmly resolved never to indulge in censure or criticism, or to entertain any wicked thoughts about anyone.

Sai would at times be pleased to confer his grace on his devotees, making them delighted. He had a unique way of granting favours to some, and at times he would bestow it amid humour and laughter! When he was pleased with someone, he would give him initiation. And once he decided to initiate someone, he would bring to that devotee a sense of fulfilment of life, and that too, quite effortlessly, through fun and laughter.

When Baba felt like blessing someone and showering him with his grace, even if he was in another country or thousands of miles away, he would bring the person to Shirdi, drawing him by his mystical power. Lakhmichand, lovingly called Lalaji, was one such blessed person to be drawn by Baba for his grace.

It was in 1910 during Christmas that Lalaji had a wonderful vision in his dream, of an old, bearded saint, surrounded by devotees, and he stood before Lalaji. With love and reverence, Lalaji paid his homage to him.

After some time, he attended a *kirtan* in Das Ganu's house where he saw Baba's photograph. He was surprised to see that it was the same saint who had appeared in his dream. Seeing it, his eyes filled with tears of joy and love, and he felt an innate longing to set his eyes on such a loving form. His eyes remained riveted on Baba's picture as he wondered if he would meet a friend who would accompany him to Shirdi. He was longing to have his *darshan*, and experience the joy of his love.

But the guru is always hungry for the love and faith of his devotee, and on that same night there was a knock at Lalaji's door. When he opened it, his friend,

Shankarrao, stood there, and asked him whether he would like to accompany him to Shirdi. Lalaji was amazed at the turn of events. He immediately consented.

They both each borrowed fifteen rupees from one of Lalaji's cousins, and caught the train to Kopergaon. Shankarrao was fond of *bhajans* and so they sang them. In between, Lalaji tried to gather information about Baba from passengers going to Shirdi, and entreating them to relate their own experiences with Baba. He spoke to four Muslims in the compartment, as they hailed from nearby Shirdi. They confirmed that Baba was a great saint who had been residing in Shirdi for many years, and he was a clairvoyant too. Soon they reached Kopergaon.

Lalaji planned to buy guavas, which were available in plenty in Kopergaon, and offer them to Baba who was very fond of them. When they reached the bank of the Godavari, the scenery was so breathtaking that he forgot all about purchasing the fruit. The *tonga* had reached the other bank of the Godavari before he remembered it, but by then it was too late. He felt sad at the remiss.

Suddenly, an old lady, with a basket on her head, approached them and asked them if they wanted guavas. To their amazement the guavas had come after them! Lalaji chose the best ones to offer Baba, and of the remaining fruits in the basket, the lady told Lalaji to offer them to Baba on her behalf.

Lalaji was filled with wonder. He had seen Baba in his dream, and then identified him when he saw Baba's photograph in Das Ganu's house. Then when he had forgotten to purchase the guavas, the old lady appeared with them. This was something truly amazing!

As they reached Shirdi they saw the flags and banners atop the mosque, and they immediately joined their hands in obeisance, with great devotion. They went to the mosque directly with the *puja* articles. As they saw Baba from a distance, they were choked with emotion.

When Lalaji had Baba's *darshan*, his mind became totally engrossed at Baba's feet. As he experienced an inner bliss, he forgot his thirst and hunger, and his surroundings. After a while, he washed Baba's feet with clean water, and performed the *puja* rituals. Then offering the flower-garland to Baba, he sat at his feet.

Baba then said, "These wretches! They sing *bhajans* on their way and ask people questions. What is there to ask others? They should see everything with their own eyes. Why should they ask other people? Can a dream so true, ever be false? Make up your mind for yourself! And where was the need to borrow money and come for *darshan*? Is your heart's desire fulfilled at least now?"

Listening to Baba's words, they were astonished. How did Baba know that they had questioned about him from others? How did he know about the dream or the borrowing of money? Oh, what marvellous intuition this was! Lalaji realised that Baba did not like anyone to borrow money for a pilgrimage or to celebrate festivals.

That day, as he sat with other devotees at Sathewada for the meal at noon, some devotee had brought *sanja* (semolina cooked in milk, sugar and ghee) and offered it to Baba as *naivedya.* This was served as *prasad* to all, and Lalaji relished it so much that he wished to have it the next day too. But this was not a daily item that was served with meals, and so his wish was unfulfilled.

But the following day, Jog arrived at the mosque with the *puja* items, and asked Baba what he would like as *naivedya.* Baba replied, "Bring a dish of *sanja* for me, while you can perform the *puja* later." So Jog went home and at once returned with the *sanja.* When the noon *arati* was performed, the devotees brought their *naivedya* to Baba. Sai said to them, "Today is a good day and I feel the *prasad* today should be of *sanja.* Bring it up here, send for it quickly! All should eat it to their hearts' content."

The devotees fetched the *sanja*, and Lalaji already started feeling hungry, though he felt some pain in his back. He became restless with the hunger and the back pain. Then he was astonished when Baba said, "It is good that you are feeling hungry. There is pain in the back which needs medicine. But the time now is for eating the *sanja.* Get ready for *arati!*" Whatever he had thought and felt, Baba had an intuitive knowledge about it. Lalaji ate to his heart's content the *sanja* that was served on his plate, and felt extremely happy that this wish too was fulfilled.

From then onwards Lalaji's devotion and love for Baba grew so much, that if he heard that anyone was going to Shirdi, he would send a garland, *dakshina,* and camphor or incense-sticks with him for Baba.

One night, while Lalaji was at Shirdi, Baba went to the Chavadi, and Lalaji went with him to see the ceremony. Suddenly, Baba had a fit of coughing, which caused him great distress and agitation. Lalaji thought, 'Oh, how troublesome is this cough! I feel as if it is the evil eye of the people that is giving rise to it!'

When Lalaji came to the mosque in the morning, Baba was seated in his usual place, and Shama was sitting before him. Baba said to Shama, "Yesterday, I had a severe bout of coughing. I really feel that someone has cast an evil eye on me. That is why this cough is troubling me in every way!"

Lalaji was amazed at how Baba could read his thoughts. With folded hands, he prayed to Baba, "Maharaj, I have been overjoyed by your *darshan*. Please be compassionate and protect me forever. Except for you, I know no other god in this world. Please bless me that I be always engrossed in worshipping you only, and experience peace and happiness." With Sai's blessings and grace, he returned home with his friend, singing Sai's praises all the way.

A lady was also fortunate to be graced by Baba. Once, she had a vision of him in her dreams, when Baba stood at her door, asking her for a meal of *khichadi* (rice and pulses cooked with spices). When she woke up, she narrated her dream to her husband who was an officer in the postal department at Burhanpur.

Soon he was transferred to Akola, and the couple decided to visit Shirdi, and have Baba's *darshan*. Arriving at Shirdi, they went straight to the mosque, and had their fill of Baba's *darshan*. They offered *puja* with devotion, and stayed on in Shirdi, happy and contented, worshipping Baba's feet every day for two months.

In the meanwhile, after fourteen days had passed, the *khichadi* still remained to be offered, the main reason for their visit to Shirdi, apart from having Baba's *darshan*. So the lady prepared the *khichadi* on the fifteenth day, and took it to the mosque. There she found that the curtains had already been drawn, behind which Baba had sat down with other devotees for the meal. Since no one could go behind the curtains, while the meal was in progress, the lady hesitated. But being impatient, having come all the way to Shirdi to offer Baba *khichadi* and being denied access to him, she just lifted the curtain, and served Baba the *khichadi*. And Baba too surprised them all. He eagerly took the *khichadi* from his plate, and lapped it up with great gusto. His devotees watched all this with great love and wonder! So the lady's dream was fulfilled to her great satisfaction.

Another blessed person was the simple Brahmin, Megha. His association with Baba from previous births brought him to Shirdi. He met Rao Bahadur Sathe purely by chance when the latter was Assistant Collector in Kheda district. Megha was immediately employed to perform the *puja* in the Shiva temple.

Sathe used to visit Shirdi quite often, and have Baba's blessings and *darshan*, his mind at once absorbed at Sai's feet. When he saw people flocking there in great hordes, he decided to build a *wada* there for people to stay in. He acquired the piece of land where Baba had first appeared, and had sat under the *neem* tree, observing total silence for a period of twelve years. Sathe soon raised a building with four verandahs. He set aside an area around the *neem* tree, where people sat to meditate.

Megha had become neglectful of certain prescribed acts and observances. But Sathe brought him back on the righteous path by initiating him into reciting the *Gayatri Mantra*. As Megha continued to serve Sathe, they became very fond of each other, and their mutual respect also grew. For Megha, Sathe was his guru for whom he harboured great devotion and affection.

One day, as they were conversing, Sathe talked to Megha about his own guru, Baba. He said, "I wish with all my heart that I can bathe Baba with the water of the holy Ganga. And it is chiefly with this intention that I'm sending you to Shirdi. And seeing your dedicated service to me, I sincerely feel that you should be blessed by Sadguru, and in his company, develop sincere faith and devotion for him. Your physical existence will then have meaning, and you will have achieved the highest good in this birth. Go and worship Sai's feet with mind, speech and action."

When Megha wanted to know about Baba's caste, even Sathe did not know it, but he said that he was a Muslim *fakir* living in a mosque. Megha's immediate reaction was rejection of worshipping Baba. He thought, 'There is no creature meaner than a Muslim. Of what worth is he as a guru?' If he refused to go, Sathe would be angry, and if he did, then he would be entering purgatory, for was he not a pure Brahmin? He was worried and anxious, and his mind restless. But Sathe insisted that he must go to Shirdi and Megha left very reluctantly.

When Megha reached the courtyard of the mosque in Shirdi, Baba, with a stern look on his face, picked up a stone, saying, "Don't you dare put your foot on the step! This is a place inhabited by a Muslim! You will be polluted. Go back, return this minute!"

Megha, like the others gathered there, trembled with fear at Baba's anger, but this anger was only an outward show, for Baba was full of compassion within. Megha was astonished to realise that Baba had known his innermost thoughts, while he had been so many miles away from Shirdi.

The anger on Baba's face intimidated Megha, and as Baba kept advancing to beat him, Megha kept retreating. This situation prevailed for a few days, but Megha was inevitably drawn to Baba, and went on serving him in whatever manner he could. But he had no conviction.

Later, when he returned home, his temperature shot up suddenly, and he became bedridden. So he returned to Shirdi, and as he came back he felt very happy, and so continued to stay on. His faith grew, and he became a steadfast devotee of Baba. Now Sai became his God. He saw in Baba pureness and divinity, and Baba became his sole object of worship.

It became Megha's habit to perform *puja* at the various temples, in a particular, fixed routine, with proper rites and rituals, and then go to the mosque. Here he would lovingly make obeisance to Baba, and after pressing his feet, he would drink the *teertha* (sacred water washed off Baba's feet). He regularly performed the noonday *arati* so long as he was in Shirdi.

One day, there was a break in his routine. In spite of all his efforts, he could not offer *puja* to Khandoba, for, try as he would, the door of the temple could not be opened. So, leaving the temple with no *puja* performed there, he came to the mosque with the *arati*. Baba at once said, "Today, there has been a break in your daily *puja*. All the other Gods have been worshipped, but one god remains without the daily *puja*. Go, perform that and then return".

When Megha said that he could not pry open the temple door, Baba told him that now that door was open. Without wasting a moment, Megha went back, and realised the truth of Baba's words. He offered *puja* to the deity, and his restless mind was soothed. Only then did Baba allow Megha to do his *puja*.

One day, on Makara Sankranti day to be precise, Megha wished to give Baba a proper bath with waters from the Godavari river, after anointing him with oil, sandalpaste, etc., and ritual ingredients for a full bath. He pestered Baba to consent, and Baba asked him to do as he pleased. So Megha at once picked up the water-vessel and set out for the Godavari river, before sunrise, without an umbrella, and barefoot.

The distance was sixteen miles each way, a long distance to traverse by foot, but this did not worry him in the least. When his resolve was firm, and there was enthusiasm to accomplish this task, where was the effort or exhaustion? A firm faith made even the toughest task very simple. He fetched the water in the copper vessel thus.

Megha kept persuading Baba to get up for a bath, but Baba did not pay heed to such advice. The noon *arati* was over, and people had returned to their homes, yet Baba would not stir from his seat. Finally, with Megha's persistence, he relented and sat down for the bath, but saying, "Really, Megha! I do not want this bath with the holy water. Oh, how foolish can you be! Why does a *fakir* like me want holy water?" But Megha was not prepared to listen to anything. He only wanted to bathe him with the holy water.

Seeing his firm resolve, unbounded love and pure heart, he said, "All right! Let your wish be fulfilled! But just sprinkle a little water over my head. Of all the parts of the body, the head is the main part. Sprinkle a little water on it, and it will be equal to a full bath. Listen to at least this request of mine!"

Megha nodded, and lifting the copper vessel, emptied the water first over Baba's head, saying "Har Gange!", and then all over Baba to give him a complete bath.

Megha was pleased with himself for having poured water all over Baba, including his clothes. But wonder of wonders! Not a drop of water had drenched Baba's clothes, and apart from his head, not a single part of Baba's body was wet! Megha, watching this in sheer amazement, realised Baba's *leela* in this, and his pride was humbled. The people standing around Baba too were greatly astonished!

Baba said to Megha, "You wished to bathe me, go ahead and do according to your wishes. But even in that you will get my sign, quite easily." Everyone can achieve his desired goal if he keeps a steady, immovable faith in his guru. Sai instructed the devotee, little by little, by giving some inner sign in the actual practical life, and by creating a fondness for the spiritual life.

Megha had a large, full-length picture of Baba, given to him by Nana, which he had placed in the *wada.* He used to perform *puja* and *arati* daily to this picture, and to Baba at the mosque. One day, while he lay on his bed with his eyes closed, his mind was fully awake, when he clearly saw Baba. Baba knew he was mentally awake, and throwing some grains of consecrated rice on his head, he said, "Megha, do draw a *trishool* (trident)," and disappeared.

Megha opened his eyes, but there was no sign of Baba, except the rice all over the bed, and the door shut as before. He was quite puzzled.

He went to the mosque at once, and after taking Baba's *darshan*, he narrated to him the *trishool* incident, and asked his permission to draw it. He then told him of the vision.

Baba said, "What vision? Did you not hear my words, telling you to draw the *trishool*? Calling it a vision, are you trying to evaluate my words? My words have a profound significance. Not even a letter in them is meaningless!"

Megha said that even he thought that Baba had woken him up, but that not a single door had been open and so he thought that it was a vision. Baba said, "No door is necessary for my entry. I have neither shape nor size. I am always everywhere. Whoever unburdens to me and becomes one with me, of him I become the controller, regulating body functions."

Megha returned to the *wada* and drew the *trishool* on the wall near Baba's picture, using red colour.

The following day, a Ramdas devotee from Poona arrived at Shirdi, and making obeisance to Baba, very lovingly offered him a Shiva-linga. Just at that moment Megha arrived and Baba said to him, "See, this Shankar has come for you. Now, you look after him." Megha was extremely delighted, for he was a great Shiva *bhakta*, and to get this *linga* soon after drawing the *trishool* was indeed the *leela* of Baba. Overwhelmed with joy and gratitude, Megha came out of the mosque, carrying the *linga* with him. Dikshit, who had finished his bath just then, and was engrossed in chanting Sai's name, suddenly had the *darshan* of the *linga.* He wondered why he should get the *darshan* of the *linga* that day while he was chanting Sai's name. No sooner had this thought come to him than he saw that Megha was standing beside him, and saying, "Look, Kaka! See, Baba has given me this *linga.*" Kaka was happy to see the *linga*, but at the same time he realised that the *darshan* he had of the *linga* a moment ago resembled this *linga.*

Later, Baba got Megha to instal the *linga* near his picture, close to the *trishool* that he had drawn. Megha, who was fond of performing Shankar *puja* was blessed by Baba with the *linga*, for his faith and devotion were firm and steadfast.

A group of four came from Madras to Shirdi to have Baba's *darshan*. They used to sing devotional songs, and were on their way to Benaras, halting on the way at Shirdi. They had heard a lot about Baba, that he was compassionate, maganimous and caring, and distributed money to those who he thought deserved it. Many artistes, devotees, pilgrims, wayfarers, etc., were fortunate to be chosen by Baba as being worthy of the money.

The troupe from Madras consisted of a husband and wife, their daughter, and the wife's sister. They took *darshan* of Baba, and felt happy and satisfied. Every day, they sang *bhajans* very lovingly in front of Baba. Their enthusiastic way of singing made Baba give them a rupee or eight *annas*, whichever came to his mind. Sometimes he gave them *burfi* (coconut sweet) worth two rupees, and sometimes nothing. But then, such was the way Baba functioned, for he did not always give to everyone in charity. It was only to one whose deserved moment had come that he would give with his blessings, thus also giving him happiness and prosperity.

Amongst the *bhajan* group from Madras only the wife had a sincere love and devotion for Sai while singing the *bhajans*. The others would sing very sweetly, seemingly full of devotion, but inwardly filled with greed for money and with the hope of securing more and more money from Baba every day.

Once, while the noon *arati* was in progress, the kind Sai saw the lady's (the wife of the leader of the Madras troupe) devotion, and gave her *darshan* in the form of Lord Rama. She felt choked with emotion, tears of joy flowing from her eyes, as she beheld the figure of her favourite deity. She clapped her hands, as the singing continued, and people were surprised to see tears rolling down her cheeks. They wondered why she seemed so overjoyed.

Later in the evening, as she described to her husband how comely and resplendent with a garland of wild flowers, a crown and earrings, Lord Rama looked as Baba gave her *darshan* as Lord Rama, he was surprised, for he had not seen anyone other than Baba. She said that she had seen Lord Rama, light-complexioned as the petals of a blue lotus, clad in a yellow raiment, the weapons in his four hands, and the precious Kaustubh (the jewel that was procured during the churning of the ocean). She added, that though Sai looked like a *fakir*, begging for alms from door to door, he was no ordinary being, for he had appeared as Lord Rama.

But the husband was not so easily convinced. He decided that women were too trusting and vulnerable, and anyway, how was it possible that Sai should appear as Rama? And how did she alone see such a phenomenon? With several such devious thoughts, he mocked her, but her spirits were not dampened.

On the same night, he had a terrible dream in

which he saw himself being arrested by a policeman, handcuffed with his hands behind, and being pulled roughly along the road. Then he was behind bars, outside which stood Baba, quietly and motionless. When he saw Baba there, he begged with folded hands and with all humility, "Baba, on hearing of your fame and name, we came to you, then why is there so much calamity when you are here?"

Baba replied, "Each one has to suffer the *karmas* that he has done!"

When the man said that he had not done any *karmas*, at least not in the present birth, Baba said it could be then the *karmas* of another birth. But the man continued to argue, that he knew nothing of the previous births, but even had he done any wrong, then how was it that Baba's *darshan* did not reduce his *karmas* to ashes, and free him from them?

Baba asked him whether he had that much faith, which the man answered in the affirmative. Then Baba asked him to close his eyes which he obeyed, and he suddenly heard a loud thud like someone falling down. He at once opened his eyes, startled, and found that he had been released from the bondage, while the policeman had fallen down, covered with blood. Baba smiled and said, as the man panicked, "You are going to be caught now! The police officers will come here, and taking you to be wild and uncontrollable, arrest you once again."

The man pleaded with Baba again, saying that

what Baba said was true, and he begged him to protect him for he saw no other protector than Baba. Baba then again told him to close his eyes. He obeyed, and when he opened them again, he found himself out of the cage with Baba standing beside him. He prostrated before Baba who said to him, "The salutation that you made just now, and the ones that you made before in the mosque, is there any difference between the two? Just think and tell me!"

The man replied, "Oh Maharaj, the difference is great, like that between heaven and earth! My salutations previously were purely out of greed for money, but now it is as to God Himself! I had no faith, and was considering you to be a Muslim who was polluting us, the Hindus!"

Baba asked, "Do you not have devotion in your mind for the deities of the Muslims?" The man answered "No." Baba then reminded him that he had the *Panja* (the iron hand representing the Mohammedan holy five personages) and *Kaad Bibi* (a chosen deity of the Muslims), which he worshipped. The man agreed, and Baba asked him what other wish he had. When he expressed his longing to have the *darshan* of his guru, Ramdas, Baba told him to look behind. When he did so, he saw his guru in person. He fell at his guru's feet, but his guru disappeared, and he began to ask Baba something out of curiosity, "Baba, you are old, your body looks old. Do you know your lifespan?"

Baba said, "What? What did you say? That I look old? Just try running with me!" So saying, Baba began to run with the man in pursuit. But Baba ran faster and faster, raising a cloud of dust in his wake, and soon vanished out of sight.

When the man woke up, his attitude towards Baba had undergone a sea-change, and he began to sing praises of Baba. He developed faith and devotion towards him, and all his earlier doubts disappeared completely. The following day, when he came to the mosque for Baba's *darshan*, Baba gave him and the others in his group *burfis* of two rupees worth. He also gave them two rupees from his pocket, and made them remain in Shirdi for some more days, giving them opportunities for his *darshan* and for singing the *bhajans*.

When they finally left Shirdi on their pilgrimage to Benaras, Baba blessed them with a good, fruitful pilgrimage, and wealth.

When people prayed to Baba with full faith, he was ever ready to help them, and even the improbable became possible. Once a couple named Raghunathrao and Savitri Tendulkar, living in Bombay, were beset with worries as their son, Babu, refused to sit for the examination. Having had the Western medical education in a medical college, Babu was filled with doubts and misgivings about his ability to pass the examination. He lacked confidence and his spirits were low, though he studied very hard till late in the night.

He consulted an astrologer about his success in the examination, and was told that only in the following year would he pass it.

The boy was extremely dejected and decided not to sit for the examination. The parents were worried, and his mother undertook a journey to Shirdi. She bowed her head at Sai's feet, and he enquired about the well-being of everybody. She told him what the astrologer had predicted, and how her son was despairing.

On hearing this Baba said, "Tell him to listen to me! Say that I have asked him to ignore all that the astrologer said, and go, appear for the exam, with his mind at rest. Tell him not to be taken in by anybody, and to carry on his studies resolutely. Tell him to repose full faith in me, and he will succeed!"

Taking leave of Baba, Savitri returned to Bombay and narrated to Babu Sai's instructions. Hearing this, the boy went to the examination hall with full confidence, and answered all the questions within the stipulated time. But once he came home, the fears again set in. He began to feel that he had fared badly, and dejection once again set in. He felt he could not tackle the oral exam.

Babu sat down dejectedly to his meal, and his friend came running over to him saying, "Oh, what a wonder of wonders! Do you know, the examiner is anxious for you and asked me why you did not come yesterday! I told him that you had failed in the written exam, and hence were sitting at home. So the examiner told me that you have passed in the written exam, and to fetch you at once for the orals."

Babu was filled with great joy and wonder. Praying to Sainath for help, he ran eagerly to appear for the oral exam. Later, everything happened for the better. He passed the exam, and his confidence in himself was once again established. Since Babu had trusted Baba, and placed faith in him, Baba came to his rescue. When faith begins to waver, then doubts start creeping in, turning to convictions, but at such times, only an unshakable and steadfast faith in the Master can make doubts disappear, and the path becomes clear.

And Sai's concern for his devotees did not stop with Babu, but extended to his father, Raghunathrao Tendulkar, too, who was very loving, generous, righteous, and greatly devoted to Sai. He had faithfully served in Bombay in a well-known trading company, and now he was old, weak of eyesight, and his various body systems were becoming feeble. So to refresh his health, he took leave, and enjoyed peace and quiet. When his leave got exhausted, he still felt he needed to improve some more, and wrote an application, requesting for an extension of the leave, which was granted.

The chief officer of the company was large-hearted and considerate, and recognising the meritorious services of the loyal and honest Raghunath, he offered him half of his salary as pension to take care of his future. But Raghunath wondered if he would actually get the mentioned pension after retirement. His salary was only hundred and fifty rupees, and his pension would amount to seventy five rupees with which he would have to sustain the family.

While there was just a fortnight for the final order of his pension to be passed, Baba appeared in a dream to his wife and asked her about the family well-being, saying, "It is my wish to give your husband hundred rupees as pension. Will that satisfy his wish?"

The lady replied, "Why do you say that, Baba? We have full faith in you alone." And very soon, a resolution was passed at Raghunath's office that he would be eligible for half his salary as pension. Though Baba had mentioned a hundred, the office added another ten rupees, and Raghunath was extremely happy and grateful to Baba for his kind-hearted gesture.

Captain Hate in Gwalior too experienced Baba's kindness and love for him. Once Baba appeared in his dream, and asked him if he had forgotten him. Hate caught Baba's feet at once and said that if the child forgot his mother, where would he find refuge? He rose at once, and going to the garden, plucked some fresh beans. He gathered some rice, pulses, flour, etc., and prepared a special offering for Baba. As he was about to set out with the basket containing the offering and some *dakshina*, he woke up from his dream.

Captain Hate immediately wanted to fulfil his dream, and go to Shirdi for it, but he could not leave Gwalior right then. So he asked his friend, Kakasaheb Dikshit, through a letter, to buy the provisions, including the best variety of beans, and offer them to Baba. Then, making his obeisance, he was to ask for the *prasad* which was to be sent to Gwalior. He told Dikshit that he would be sending him the money for all the expenses.

When the money did arrive, Dikshit purchased all the ingredients, but to his consternation, the beans were not available. Suddenly, a lady carrying a basket of vegetables, happened to pass by, and she carried with her a good variety of beans! This astonished everyone, for it was not available anywhere else. Such is Sai's *leela*.

These were carried to the mosque and offered to Baba. He gave them to Nimonkar who cooked them and brought them the following day as *naivedya.*

Later, when Baba sat down for his meal, he touched neither the *daal* nor the rice, but made a meal of the beans. When Hate heard about this, he was overwhelmed with joy!

One day, he had a great longing to possess a coin that was consecrated by Baba. Once such a good desire arises in a devotee, due to Sai's benevolence and grace, it does not take even a moment for it to materialise. At that very moment one of Hate's friends appeared, saying that he was going to Shirdi. Hate gave him a coin, saying, "Do not forget to put it in Baba's hands."

When the friend reached Shirdi, he went to the mosque for Baba's *darshan.* He bowed at his feet reverentially, and then sat in front of him. When Baba put his hand out for *dakshina,* he offered his own coin first, which Baba pocketed at once. Then he offered Hate's coin to baba, saying, "Doctor Hate has sent this *dakshina* with me for you".

Baba, dwelling in all hearts, knew of Hate's desire, and sat gazing at the coin. Overwhelmed with love, he kept on staring at it, while everyone sat, wondering what Baba's plans were. Baba then tossed it with his right thumb in the air, catching it again in his hand. He repeated it every now and then, and then returned it to Hate's friend, saying, "Give this back to him to whom it belongs. Give him this *udhi* also. And tell him we do not want anything of his! Be at ease."

The friend prostrated before Baba, and then returned to Gwalior. When he returned the sanctified coin to Hate, the latter was overwhelmed with joy and love. Baba's ways were rather mysterious, for though he pocketed one coin given by one person, he returned another coin given to him by another person! Only he knows his reasons.

Once Vaman Narvekar, an ardent devotee of Sai, offered Baba a coin of one rupee with great devotion and love. On one side of the coin were engraved the figures of Rama, Sita and Lakshmana, and on the other side, the figure of Maruti. Vaman wanted Baba to sanctify the coin by his touch, and then return it to him, but Baba pocketed it silently.

Shama told Baba that Vaman wished for the coin, and pleaded with him to return it. But Baba refused, saying that it should be kept with themselves. Then he said that if Vaman gave him twenty five rupees, then he would return the coin. So Vaman hastily gathered together the sum from various places and gave them to Baba. Baba pocketed these too as before, saying, even if hoards of rupees were fetched, they would not weigh as this coin, nor would their value be more.

Baba turned to Shama, and said, "Take this for you, Shama! Let it be in your collection. Keep it in the shrine and worship daily." Who indeed knows Baba's ways!

Anyone who receives Baba's grace will enjoy power, inconceivably great, and the treasure of discriminating knowledge between the self and the non-self, and with that will come Enlightenment. Sai knows the wishes of his devotees very well, and satisfies them too if he deems them worthwhile!

Once, the wife of Sakharam Aurangabadkar came to Shirdi for Baba's *darshan*. She had no issues, and having heard of the greatness of Sai Baba, she came there with her stepson. She was tired of making vows to the various gods and goddesses, for even after twenty seven years of marriage, she was barren.

But a doubt arose, even as she came to Shirdi. How would she talk to him in privacy, when Baba was always surrounded by his devotees? How could she convey her heart's desire to him in front of everyone? But she stayed in Shirdi with her son for two months, hoping to corner Baba some time. Then she entreated Shama to convey her ardent wish to Baba, for he was never alone, and she could not approach him.

Shama categorically told her that it was impossible to find Baba alone, for someone or the other was always coming there for Baba's *darshan*. Baba was always accessible to all, and no one was debarred from coming to see him. But he said that he would definitely try to help her, for it was only He who decided what is best, and gives peace to those who deserve it. Then he instructed her to sit in the *sabhamantap* below, on a stone, with a coconut and incense sticks in her hand when Baba sat down for his meal. After his meal, when he was in a pleased mood, he would signal to her, and then she could come and see Baba.

Such an opportunity did come one day. After Baba had finished his meal, he washed his hands, and Shama stood beside him, wiping dry his hands. Baba was in a cheerful mood, and with a sudden outburst of love, he pinched Shama's cheek. Pretending to be angry, Shama asked Baba if this was really proper. "We do not want a mischievous God who squeezes the cheek so hard! Are we, in any way, under obligation to you? Is this the fruit of our intimacy with you?"

Baba replied, "In all these seventy two generations of our association, have I even touched you with my hand? Just try to remember!"

Shama, still feigning anger, said, "We do not want your honours. We want a God who will always give new sweetmeats to each of us when we are hungry. Give me this one gift only—that I remain grateful to you forever."

Baba assured him that only for this purpose he came there and began to feed them all, because of the tender affection he felt for him. Then he went and sat near the railing. At a signal from Shama, the lady came hastily up the steps, and stood before Baba in great humility and reverence. She offered him the coconut, and bowed at his feet. Baba banged the coconut against the railing with his own hands, and then asked Shama what that coconut was conveying, for it was rattling too much. Shama told Baba to place the coconut in her lap and bless her with children.

Baba, in mock horror, said to the lady, "What, do coconuts produce children? How do you allow such superstitions to control your senses? People seem to have gone crazy!"

Shama intervened, and playfully scolding Baba, said, "Oh, well we know the power and wonder of your words, but you are arguing needlessly. Oh, give her that coconut as *prasad*!"

Baba said. "All right, break the coconut!" But Shama said, "Oh, give it in her lap first," and this argument continued for a while, after which Baba ultimately gave in, and blessing the lady, said, "She will get a child. Now go!" But Shama wanted to know when, and on his persistence, Baba said, twelve months. Shama broke the coconut, and while he gave one half to her, the other half he shared with Baba.

Later, Shama assured her that Baba always fulfilled the wishes of anyone who surrendered to him wholeheartedly and totally. He said that if, within twelve months, she did not deliver a child, he would bang the coconut in the same way on Baba's head, and send him away from the mosque. He too would give up his own name. And true to his words, she did bear a child before a year was over. When the child was five months old, she brought him along with her husband to Shirdi for Sai's *darshan.* Her husband bowed at Baba's feet with great humbleness, and offered five hundred rupees to Baba as *dakshina.* Baba accepted the amount, and later used it to build the walls of the place where his horse, Shamakarna, was tied.

Bapusaheb Buty had the good fortune to be associated with Baba in many ways. Baba was very affectionate and loving towards Buty, a very wealthy person hailing from Bombay. Buty too was an ardent devotee of Baba, and he was always absorbed at his feet. He came there with his family, and continued to stay on in Shirdi, serving Baba for a long time. He felt like staying there permanently, and so bought a plot of land in Shirdi.

Even as he was contemplating building a house to reside in whenever he was in Shirdi, he had an interesting vision while he slept in the upper storey of Dikshitwada. Shama, who too was sleeping in the same *wada*, had a vision, to the astonishment of both.

Buty had a dream in which Baba ordered him to build his *wada*, most certainly including in it a temple. And immediately he woke up, trying to remember the dream from its commencement, as he lay in bed. Suddenly he heard Shama weeping, and as Buty called out to him, Shama woke up from his dream.

Shama told Buty that he was overcome with love when he heard Baba's loving words, "Let the *wada* and temple take a concrete shape. I shall fulfil the wishes of all." Shama's throat was choked with emotions, as his eyes filled with tears of love and joy. The intense love in his heart was overwhelming, making him burst into tears.

Buty was surprised that both of them should have got the same vision and instructions. They quickly drafted a plan which had the approval of Kakasaheb Dikshit.

Next morning, in the early hours, as the three of them gathered in front of Baba, Sai scrutinised Shama's face with great attention and love.

Shama said, "Oh God! What is this incomprehensible play of yours? You do not even allow us to have a peaceful sleep, for, there too you make us rave wildly." Baba at once put both his hands on his ears, and said, "Whatever anyone may say, we have been in our own places!"

Baba gave his permission for the construction of the *wada* with a temple in it. Shama saw to the construction of the basement and the ground floor, with a well outside. Baba watched the progress eagerly, as he walked to and from Lendi Bagh. While the windows and doors were being fixed, Baba gave some suggestions which would enhance the beauty of the *wada*.

Then the work was entrusted to Bapusaheb Jog. Buty was inspired to have a *sanctum sanctorum* built in the *wada*, in which could reside an idol of Muralidhar (Lord Krishna). But without consulting Baba, he did not like to take any step. So he approached Shama for his advice.

They waited for Baba to come near the *wada* while on his daily round. When Baba came, they suggested to him that both the walls dividing the hall be demolished, and an idol of Muralidhar be installed there. A quadrangle in the centre of the *wada* would be the ideal place to have a throne on which could be installed Muralidhar, but Baba's permission was necessary.

Baba happily said, "All right. Once the temple is

ready, we too will come there to stay. When the *wada* is complete, it can be used only for us," and he gazed at the *wada* lovingly. Then he added, "For there itself we will move about and talk; there we will all play, and embracing each other lovingly, enjoy infinite happiness."

Then Shama asked if the time was auspicious, and when Baba nodded, he broke the coconut. Then, in course of time, the *sanctum sanctorum* with the raised platform for Muralidhar was ready. The making of the idol of Muralidhar was entrusted to an artisan.

But as things would have it, Baba's health rapidly deteriorated, and he grew very weak. All the devotees were greatly agitated. They wondered if Baba's feet would touch the temple after all. Buty was very sad indeed to see Baba in such a frail condition. But to his great astonishment, Baba did come to occupy the *wada*. When Baba left his mortal coils, his clear injunction to his devotees was, "Please take me to the *wada*," and the sacred body of Sai was laid in the *sanctum sanctorum*. The *wada* became the *samadhi mandir,* and Baba occupied the place that was for Muralidhar, signifying very subtly that he was Muralidhar. Blessed is Buty indeed for Sai's grace.

Sapatnekar was a lawyer in Akkalkot, who became an ardent devotee of Baba, but not before a very trying time. As he was studying for law, he exchanged notes with another student named Shevade. Other students also joined in to test one another's knowledge of the subject. Shevade was not able to answer the questions correctly, and the students wondered how he would ever pass the exam.

Shevade, though being derided by them, had full faith in Sai Baba, and said to them that when the time came, he would pass. Even if he was not thorough, Baba would be there to pass him, so why should be worry?

Sapatnekar was curious to know who this Baba was, in whom his friend could repose so much faith. So he called him aside, and asked him who this Sai Baba was, whose virtues he praised so much, and in whom he had so much trust, and where did he live? Shevade gave him all the details of this famous and virtuous man. Then he told him that not only would he pass this exam, but also the next one. Sapatnekar believed this to be vain and ridiculous bragging, but later, he was astonished to see that Shevade had indeed passed both exams.

After ten years lapsed, misfortune struck Sapatnekar, causing him great distress and anxiety. His only son died of diphtheria, and he began to be disgusted with life. So he went on a pilgrimage to many holy places like Pandharpur, Gangapur, etc. But the agitation and restlessness in him continued. He then began reading the *Vedanta*. Some time passed thus, but peace was still elusive.

Then he suddenly remembered Shevade's account

of Sai Baba, and his steadfast faith in him. He felt that he should go to Shirdi and have Baba's *darshan*. So he set out with his family and his younger brother for Shirdi.

When they reached Shirdi, they had *darshan* of Baba, though from a distance, but they felt satisfied. As their eyes met Baba's across the distance, they quickly folded their hands in obeisance and approached him quickly. Prostrating before Baba with great humility, they offered a coconut at his feet with hearts filled with pure love and devotion. But Baba turned away scornfully, saying, "Get out!" Sapatnekar was taken aback, and decided to ask someone the reason for Baba's anger against him. But whom to approach? Someone suggested Bala Shimpi, the tailor.

So Sapatnekar went in search of Bala Shimpi. When he met him, he recounted to him his meeting with Baba, and suggested that if Bala accompanied him, he might get his *darshan* in peace, and Sai might bestow his grace on them without anger. Bala consented and a relieved Sapatnekar purchased a photo of Baba.

When they approached Baba again, Bala Shimpi took Baba's photo from Sapatnekar and giving it to Baba, said, "What is this picture, Oh God?"

Baba looked at it, and replied, "This is a photo of his friend," pointing out to Sapatnekar. Then he smiled, and everyone around too joined him in smiling. Bala wanted to know the meaning of all this. Baba told Sapatnekar, "Take *darshan*, be quick!" But as he made his obeisance, he heard the words, "Get out!" once again. He was again disillusioned and perplexed, wondering at Baba's anger. As he stood with Bala with folded hands before Baba, Sainath commanded them to leave at once. They entreated him to look upon them kindly and give them their blessings. They said that Sapatnekar, having heard so much about Baba, had come all the way for his *darshan*, and he needed Baba's blessings for more of his *darshan*. They went back to their village without delay.

One more year passed, and Sapatnekar's mind was still in pursuit of peace. He went to Madhegaon for rest, and then decided to go to Benaras. Two days before his journey, his wife had a dream, and their journey was stayed. She saw a *fakir*, who had a piece of cloth wrapped round his head, standing near a *neem* tree, as she was going to the well of Lakkadhsa with a pitcher. The *fakir* told her that he would fill up her pitcher fully with pure, clean water, and she need not toil so heard. But, being frightened of him, she turned back homewards, with him following her. Just then she woke up.

They both decided to pay a visit to Shirdi. On arrival there, they made their way to the mosque. Baba had gone to the Lendi, and they sat there, waiting for him. When he returned, she was amazed to see that the *fakir* in her dreams was Baba. When Baba's feet were washed, she came to him for *darshan,* and made obeisance at his feet. She sat and gazed at him in wonder. Baba was delighted by her devout conduct, and in a soft voice, he started narrating a tale to those around him, which was actually the story of the lady's affliction and how she was cured.

Baba said, "My hands, stomach, waist, all have been aching severely for many days. I am tired of trying out medicines. The ailment just does not go, and the medicines are ineffective. But I am surprised that now the ailments have all suddenly disappeared."

As the lady heard it with rapt attention, she knew that Baba was relating her story. As Baba said, after a month or two, she was cured of her afflictions. The lady's wish was fulfilled, and she was overwhelmed with joy and gratitude.

It was now the turn of Sapatnekar and when he took his *darshan* of Baba, he was once again ordered to get out! Sapatnekar was extremely perplexed and sad, for he was the only one to whom Baba did not bestow his grace. Probably, thought Sapatnekar, Baba was angry for some sins of his past, and for entertaining doubts about him in the early days. He thought that this was probably Baba's way of drawing him closer. So he decided to stay on in Shirdi till he was blessed with Baba's grace.

He remained in Shirdi, concentrating his mind on Baba, but that day, he felt very sad. He could not relish his food, and he lay on his bed, eyes wide open. He decided to go to the mosque the following day, and when there was nobody around, he would fall at Baba's feet, and clinging to the feet, seek his blessings.

So, the following day, when the opportunity came, he fell at Baba's feet, and bowing his head, placed them on the hallowed feet. Baba placed his hand on Sapatnekar's head. The devotee began to press his guru's feet when a shepherdess arrived there. She immediately sat down to massage Baba's waist vigorously, and Baba, as usual, began talking to her.

As Sapatnekar listened in silence, he gradually realised that Baba was talking about him to her. Every detail that he described seemed to conform to his life, right from the birth of his son to his death. Though Baba seemed to be telling the shepherdess of a person who was not present there, Sapatnekar realised that he was subtly alluding to his life story. As he listened, his reverence for Baba grew, and he started regarding him as one who is one with Brahman, and his admiration multiplied. Truly, Baba was very intuitive. Just then Baba spoke, pointing his finger at Sapatnekar, "I have killed his child, he says. He has accused me of this. If I kill people's children, then why does he come to the mosque and weep? All right, now I will bring his child back as his son."

On hearing this, Sapatnekar's eyes filled with tears of joy. As he sat there, gazing lovingly at Baba, Sainath placed his hand on his head, and said, "These feet are very ancient. All your care is removed. Have full faith and trust in me, and soon your wishes will be fulfilled."

Sapatnekar's tears of joy washed Baba's feet, and once again Baba blessed him with peace and joy. After the *puja* and *arati* were over, he placed the *naivedya* plate in front of Baba, offering it to him. He felt very happy when Baba consecrated it with his hand. And when people came to pay their obeisance, he too joined the crowd, and once again stood in front of Baba. Bowing at his feet, he banged his head, till Baba assured him that one salutation was enough.

Sapatnekar participated in the *chavadi* procession that night. And as he looked at Baba, he found himself gazing at Panduranga of Pandharpur! He was extremely pleased and choked with emotion at this wonder.

Later, when he went to Baba to seek his permission for departure, Baba suggested to him to have his meal, rest awhile, and then go. Before going, Sapatnekar wished to have Baba's *darshan*. Suddenly a doubt arose. If Baba asked for *dakshina*, what was he to do, for he had just enough for the return journey. He decided that he would give Baba one rupee even before his asking, and if he asked again, he would give another rupee. But were he to ask for more, then he would have to tell Baba frankly just how much he had.

With this resolve, he went to the mosque for Baba's *darshan*. He placed a rupee in Baba's hand,

and when Baba asked for more, he handed over another rupee. Then Baba said quite clearly, "Take this coconut and put it on your wife's lap. Then you may leave peacefully, and forget all your restless agitation." Sapatnekar bowed and took his leave.

After a year, a son was born to the couple. When the child was eight months old, they brought him to Shirdi and placed him at Baba's feet. Baba blessed them all, and to Sapatnekar's great delight later, two more sons were born to him.

One's first impression of Sai Baba was of his magnetic and experienced eyes. There was such power and penetration in his gaze that none could hold his gaze for long. One felt that he was looking into one's inner being, reading everything. One felt that he penetrated into the very core of the being, into every single atom in the body. A few words or a gesture would signify to one that Sai Baba was aware of all about the past, the present and the future. One was helpless to do anything else other than submit trustfully and surrender oneself to him. And he was always there to take care of every minute detail, guiding one through every vicissitude of life, and showering his precious grace on one. Indeed, blessed are those fortunate ones who receive Sainath's grace!

6

Sai's Clairvoyance

Baba was often heard repeating 'Allah Malik hai' ceaselessly, and would often indulge in a *naam-saptah* (a week-long chanting of the name) with his devotees who would sit before him and chant the name day and night continuously.

Once, Das Ganu was asked to start a *naam-saptah*, and he consented with the condition that Vittal must appear before him. Baba assured him saying that Vittal would appear in form if only the devotee had enough faith. He added, "Dankapuri of Dakurnath, or Pandharpur of Vittalraya, or Dwarka of Ranchchod—everything is in Shirdi itself. You do not have to seek far. After all, Vittal, moved by the intense love of his devotees, will incarnate in this very place for you." When the *saptah* came to an end, Das Ganu did have the *darshan* of Vittal. So true were Baba's words!

Once while Kakasaheb Dikshit was meditating after his early morning bath, he was blessed with the vision of Vittal. Filled with immense joy, he told Baba about the vision. Baba instructed him, "Hold on to that Vittal fast and fix him in place forcibly, for he is very elusive and can give you the slip if you are inattentive even for a moment."

At noon, some villagers came to Shirdi to sell a few pictures of Vithoba of Pandharpur. Dikshit was stunned to see the resemblance of these pictures with the vision he had had! Purchasing one, he installed it in his *puja* room with great love and reverence, remembering Baba's words.

Once while Baba was sitting in the mosque, a devotee heard a lizard chirping incessantly. He asked Baba the significance of the noise. Baba said to him, "The lizard is overwhelmed with joy that her sister is coming here from Aurangabad to meet her."

The devotee, surprised to hear such an answer, decided that Baba must have said it to create some humour: Some time later, a rider from Aurangabad arrived there to have Baba's *darshan*. Baba was engaged in having a bath. The rider decided to go to the market to buy fodder for his horse. When he removed the horse's mouth-bag from under his arm, and shook it thoroughly to empty it out, there dropped from the bag a lizard! It slid swiftly across the floor with great fear. Baba said to the devotee, "Now, keep a careful eye on her! This indeed is the sister of that lizard. Just watch this marvel!"

The sister soon joined the other lizard on the wall, who was already chirping noisily and incessantly. They hugged and embraced each other, celebrating their union! The devotee sat there stupefied. Where was Aurangabad, where Shirdi! And how Baba had explained the significance of the incessant chirping! Had the devotee not been there, or not asked Baba about it, how would Sai's greatness have been revealed?

Once a man called Mamledar sent a basket of the famous Alphonso mangoes to Baba, addressed to Shama (Madhavrao). When the basket was opened in front of Baba, three hundred delicious mangoes were in it. Baba looked at them and handed over everything to Shama, who put four in the earthen vessel and carried the rest home.

As the fruit fell into the earthen vessel, Baba said, "This fruit is for Damuanna; let it lie there." Two hours later, when Damuanna came to see Baba with flowers for Baba's *puja* Baba said cryptically, "The mangoes are Damya's. They are not ours, though people are eager to grab them. Only he should have them to whom they belong. Why should we want another's things? Only he should eat them to whom they belong—even if he dies eating them!"

Anna accepted them as *prasad* with full faith in Baba. After *puja*, he went home but returned to ask Baba to which of his wives he should give the fruit. Baba said, "Give them to the younger. The marvel of these mangoes will bring forth four sons and four daughters."

Anna, who had given up hopes of ever having children, was extremely pleased with Baba's words. In course of time, what Baba had said came to transpire. His blessings bore fruit, and Damuanna had eight children.

Baba once returned from the Lendi and sat in the mosque amongst devotees. Chandorkar too sat there with his brother-in-law, Biniwale. They made obeisance to Baba, and while Baba was enquiring about their well-being, he suddenly flew into a rage, shouting, "Nana, how could you forget this? Is this all that you have learnt after spending days with me? You have been in my company, and is this all it has come to in the end? Oh, how could your mind be so deluded! Tell me everything carefully."

Nana could not understand the cause of Baba's anger, and became very agitated. Baba would never hurt anyone's feelings unless something had happened. So he fell at Baba's feet, and implored him to tell him why Baba was angry.

Baba said, "When you have been in my company for years together, why should the state of your mind be still such? When did you reach Kopergaon, and what happened on the way? Did you alight anywhere or did you drive the *tonga* straight here? Did anything unusual happen on the way? I wish to hear every detail, even if it is trivial."

Nana's face fell and he felt ashamed to tell all, but he did narrate everything as it happened. They had hired the *tonga* to go straight to Shirdi, but then Biniwale would have missed the *darshan* of Shri Datta on the banks of the Godavari. But Nana was in a hurry to reach Shirdi and suggested that they could visit Shri Datta on their return journey. While they were bathing in the Godavari, a thorn got lodged in Nana's foot, and with tremendous effort he got it out.

Baba warned Nana that this time he had been let off with only a thorn. When a tutelar deity like Datta was waiting on the way to give *darshan*, to have ignored him did not please Baba. Nana, knowing Baba's clairvoyance, was not surprised that he had known all that had occurred.

Once Ramachandra Patil of Shirdi became very ill, and suffered greatly. He tried all cures but there was no change in his health. While he was in this state, Baba appeared at his bedside one night. Patil clasped his feet and entreated him to reveal when he would die, for he was tired of life.

Baba said to him with compassion, "Do not worry. The imminent danger from your dreaded sickness is already overcome. Why do you worry unnecessarily? For you there is absolutely no fear. But, Oh Ramachandra, I see no hope for Tatya Patil. In the year 1918, in the month of *Ashwin* (October), on Vijayadashami day, Tatya will go to his Eternal Abode. But do not tell him of this."

Only two years remained for Tatya's end, and

Ramachandra was worried. He did not disclose his fear to him, but only to Bala Shimpi, entreating him to keep it a closely guarded secret.

When in 1918, the Ashwin month began, Tatya fell ill and took to bed. He had high fever, but Baba in the mosque began to shiver with cold. Tatya could hardly get up from his bed to go for Baba's *darshan*.

Baba's condition was becoming worse, as he groaned and moaned. He was growing weaker day by day, and his ailment became uncontrollable.

Soon the day that Baba had predicted drew near. Bala Shimpi became apprehensive and broke into cold sweat. So did Ramachandra Patil. They realised that Baba's words were materialising as Tatya lay dying. Viajayadashami day dawned, but something unexpected happened. While Tatya recovered, it was Baba who left his mortal coils. He had taken Tatya's name, but was actually preparing for his own *samadhi*. And yet he had given the warning, alerting everyone of the future event.

On the day after Baba took *samadhi*, Das Ganu had a dream in which Baba appeared and instructed him, "The mosque has crumbled down. All the grocers and oil merchants of Shirdi have harassed me. So I am now going away from there and have come here. Cover me up with a profusion of flowers. Oh, do fulfil this wish of mine. Come immediately to Shirdi!" Before he left, he came to know of Baba's *mahasamadhi*, and set out post-haste to Shirdi.

Baba always gave a warning of things to come, much in advance, surprising people. For many years together, he had used the brick that had hurt his guru, Venkusha's head. While he sat in *yogasana,* he took the support of that brick. This practice had gone on without interruption for a long time.

One day, while Baba was absent from the mosque, a young boy, Abdul by name, who served Baba devotedly, lifted the brick to sweep under it. The brick, destined to break, slipped from his fingers and fell with a crash, breaking into two.

When Baba heard this, he said, "It is not the brick, but fortune that is broken." His eyes filled with tears of sorrow, his heart torn with grief. The life-companion seemed to have been plucked from him, leaving him forlorn. But he knew now that his life in human form was soon to end.

Once Jog asked Baba, that in spite of serving Baba single-mindedly, why did his fickle mind have no rest? Baba told him lovingly, "I will consider you of great fortune only when all your sins are burnt to ashes, and when I see a bag under your arm for collecting alms. I will regard as truly fortunate, when all delusions created by *maya* are relinquished, and a fond detachment is developed. When you have conquered all your desires, then will I think of you as fortunate."

By his grace, Jog attained that detachment that Baba had spoken about, and he soon renounced everything before leaving his body.

Anandrao had implicit faith in Baba, spurning riches rather than this faith. And he remained resolute till his end. Baba had said to him, "Your faith and loyalty will bear fruit. I will send you an aeroplane and take you away on it. Have not a care in your mind!" Baba's words of benediction did bear fruit, for he passed away very peacefully without a care in the world.

Baba's love for his devotees was without bounds. In fact, he looked on all creatures as equal. He was one with them at heart. While returning from the Lendi, if he met goats, he would feel elated. He would look at them lovingly, sometimes resting his eyes on a couple or two. He would purchase them and keep them with Kondaji.

One day, Baba purchased two goats for Rs. 32. While everyone was surprised, he patted them lovingly on their backs. He remembered his association with them in their previous birth, and was overcome with love. On seeing them born as goats, he felt pity for them.

Tatya was flabbergasted to know that Baba had paid so much for the goats which would otherwise cost about three or four rupees. Shama too joined him in protesting against Baba's action. They were indignant with Baba who, they felt, had been deceived. Baba though was calm and unruffled. They asked him humbly why he had paid so much for the goats. Baba smiled and said, "Truly crazy are these people! Oh, how will I make them understand?" Yet he remained composed and happy. Those who have the power of discriminating knowledge will never be aroused to anger.

On their insistence, Baba told them, "I, who have no place even to sit, and no home, why should I want possessions? Go to the shop first, and buy a measure of pulse. Feed this to the goats and then return them to the shepherd."

They obeyed his command, and returned after performing the tasks. The money had gone with the goats who had been returned to their owner! They wondered at this strange deed of Baba.

Baba narrated to them the following story. In their previous birth, the goats were human beings. The goats were then brothers who fought among themselves, and hence they had to suffer their *karma*.

In the beginning the brothers were very fond of each other, and there was a strong bond of love between them. But gradually, greed for money created a rift. While the elder brother idled away his time, the younger one worked hard day and night and reaped great wealth. Their egos brought about enmity between them, and they soon were at loggerheads with each other. Finally, they killed each other and to work out their *karma*, they were born as goats. Seeing them suddenly, Baba was overcome with love for them.

Baba thought that by spending money out of his pocket, he would give them respite, but in the form of

Shama and Tatya, their *karma* stood in the way. Baba was filled with compassion for them, but on the insistence of Shama and Tatya, he gave in, and returned the goats to their owner. Truly, Sainath was compassionate as well as clairvoyant.

S.B. Mohile had a daughter with a harelip. He took her to Baba for cure, but Baba warned him, "She is of divine nature, and her life is short-lived. She will die on the next Chaturthi day. If you attend office on that day, you will not see her again." True to his words, it happened as Baba had predicted. She died while her father was at work on Chaturthi day. Baba, who was omniscient and all-pervading, knew what would happen and when. No doubt, he was far-seeing and a clairvoyant.

7

Sustainable Directions

"If only you will utter 'Sai, Sai' all the time, I will, with my grace, present you even the seven seas (protect you beyond the seven seas). Trust these words of mine, and you will achieve your welfare, most certainly. I do not need either all the elaborate articles of *puja*, or the ceremonies or rites of *puja.* Where there is boundless faith, I abide there." So spoke Sai Baba. These pearls of wisdom will benefit mankind if only one reposes utter faith in him and seeks his guidance.

Baba's teachings were simple, and even a layman could follow them without hesitation. For a layman, he advocated the *bhakti marga* (the path of devotion) wherein the worshipper had to be wholly devoted to him, chanting the name, and serving God with love. He showed by parables the importance of identifying the guru with God, that it was seeing God in and through the guru. The guru is the medium to realise your self. If you repose faith in him and surrender to him totally so that even your body ceases to be yours, he will take charge of your ship and steer it across the ocean of life.

He who does not feel that 'I am different, people are different,' who sees this world as one, filled with the one and same spirit, finds that there is nothing which is separate from himself. To give up any idea of duality is itself to become Infinity.

Baba said, "I alone am; there is not a place where I am not; I pervade all the ten directions. Nothing exists apart from me." This is one idea which each one of us must hold on to. Even the slightest trace of duality in the mind will destroy this complete Oneness, and at once create a sense of differentiation that brings about the cause of births and deaths.

Infinity is the object of knowledge, and the Being is one who tries to get this Knowledge. When the darkness of ignorance is dispelled, the illusion of duality disappears at once, and the vision is filled with Oneness of the Self with everything else. When pure water gets mixed with pure water, they merge to become one, and are inseparable, without a trace of difference. When logs of different shapes and sizes are burnt together, they lose their separateness, their shapes combining into one mass as fire. Likewise, the *Atman*, dwelling in all living creatures, is always without a form.

While the soul is indestructible, the body is destructible. The *Atman* is a great power, but more subtle and manifest is *maya*. And subtler than both these is the *Purush* where all sense organs repose. This is the ultimate destination of all. The *Atman*, unblemished and pure as crystal, is unchangeable, but appears to be bonded to worldly life by *maya* and one's *karma.* Just as a coiled rope appears like a snake from a distance, similarly, to the *Atman* the ego that "I am the body" creates an illusory bondage.

The fulfilment of life and life's ultimate goal is consistency, fearlessness, emancipation, independence, and attainment of God. Without knowledge, there is no liberation, and without renunciation knowledge cannot be attained. But the thought of renunciation does not arise as long as this worldly life does not appear transient to the mind. One has to gain knowledge through experience and be one with everything. Only then is realisation possible.

Sai Baba advocated the greatness of knowledge above everything else, but he also advised the devotees to follow the path of devotion and recitation of the Name. He also said that meditation was the best way of snapping ties with the worldly life.

Baba also advised everyone to practise forbearance. This, he said, is the essence of manliness that overcomes sin, suffering and adversity; it also helps to drive away all fears and disasters. Forbearance or patience alone succeeds. It is a mine of virtue and the queen of virtuous thought.

Sai alone is to us the Supreme Being; in Him is our ultimate and highest goal. He is beyond the pair of opposites like joy and sorrow, love and anger, etc., and is always absorbed in the Self; and is forever, the

Ultimate Reality. He enjoys unlimited glory, and with the power of his glance can transform a pauper into a wealthy man. He is that Infinity in human form who, himself having experienced it, brings people a perception of God in a Vision, and causes action, himself remaining out of it.

While the body is in the five elements, and is destructible, the spirit is free and indestructible, and is without a beginning and an end. It is this pure Life-force, or the Ultimate, that is called 'Sai'. Himself being beyond the bodily organs, he yet controls the gross physical organs. There is no place which is without this Sai Power, pervading all the ten directions, the animate and the inanimate. After completing his mission with a form and name, he has now merged with the Unmanifest again. He dwells inside and outside forever, in you and me, in all. He is compassionate to the poor and the meek, and is the Protector of this cosmic family.

If one constantly meditates on Sai's manifest form, with all its attributes, the manifest form will disappear, and the subtle, true Self will appear. Unless one enters through the manifest form, it is not possible to know the true Self, and it becomes difficult to know the formless Infinity completely. Once the mind is completely filled with Sai, whether in the waking or dreaming or sleeping state, it is the state of renouncing the worldly life.

Baba always told his followers to have control over their senses, saying that he who had a longing for sensual pleasures could never hope to attain spiritual progress. By offering the sense objects at the guru's feet, the mind gets liberated and the sense-desires weaken. Instead there arises a love for the guru, and from here sprouts pure knowledge. As this pure knowledge grows, the bondage of bodily awareness gets severed. the same intellect now dives deep into the consciousness that "I am Brahman". It is then that one experiences bliss. Though the body is transient, it is the only way of achieving the highest goal of human existence, leading to *bhakti yoga*.

A human being exists with his ego of scant knowledge, while the all-knowing Sai is egoless. To realise the oneness between the two, the guru is the only means.

The ways of the guru are contrary to those of the world. This knowledge is gained through experience. Here, faith alone is one's sustenance, and the guru's grace is the only means. A devotee, by virtue of his own loving devotion will never boast of his knowledge, but offer his mind, body and wealth at his guru's feet. The profound nature of the Self, which the body, sense-organs, mind or the intellect cannot comprehend, is revealed to us by the grace of the guru. And to attain *moksha*, the highest goal, one needs the guru's grace.

Our hearts must be purified if we have to cross the ocean of worldly life. The source of this purification lies in devotion to God. There is no better devotion than listening to the stories of the guru which inspires love for him quite easily and effortlessly. The mind becomes cleansed and purified. And from there spirituality is born.

When you keep repeating Sai's name, sins are destroyed; *rajas* and *tamas* disappear, while *sattva* remains and grows, leading to moral and religious merit. This awakens God-devotion and moral consciousness, the sensual desires are totally destroyed, and Self-realisation happens instantly. When knowledge is gained through a discriminating intelligence, the whole concentration is on Self-absorption, which in itself means remaining humbly at the guru's feet. This is known as complete surrender to the guru.

Though the guru might appear to be stern, he is full of love for his devotee. One should therefore have patience and courage in one's heart, and he will work for your weal in the end. When one is in the guru's company, misfortunes, attachment and self-interests disappear. One should therefore surrender to one's guru without conceit, but with humility and a prayer. If one follows a true guru, one will be liberated, such being the inconceivable power of the guru!

There are two ways of gaining the favour of one's guru: one is devotion, and the other is *jnana*. The path of devotion is easy while the *jnana-marga* is arduous. Though by comparison, the path of devotion is not arduous, yet one needs a succession of meritorious births to meet one's guru, and it is only then that one enjoys the happiness of the guru's company, which fosters devotion.

Without love, knowledge is dry and of no use to anyone, nor is there any satisfaction. One needs to have deep love in the heart to make all the listening and reading fruitful. And in love resides true devotion, peace, renunciation and liberation. But love arises only with faith, and where there is faith, there is God.

If one can discriminate between the transient and the eternal, give up the desire for the fruit in this world and the next, and practise the basic disciplines enumerated in the *Vedas* and the *Upanishads*, one will finally attain *moksha*.

The world being transient, meditate wholly upon the guru which leads to spiritual progress. By abandoning the transient, one develops detachment. The universal consciousness of the Brahman fills the Sadguru, and the presence of God is felt in all the living creatures. This is known as the worship of Non-duality. By constantly meditating upon the guru, a devotee becomes one with his guru. With single-minded meditation and *sadhana*, the consciousness of the body is completely forgotten, the awareness of the worldly life disappears, and only the bliss of Self-absorption is experienced. Hence, go on repeating the name of your guru.

Baba always made his meaning clear, either by simple words that a layman could follow, or by events or miracles. Just as the grandeur of a dream-kingdom disappears on waking up, so will the illusory quality of this worldly life, said Baba. Given below are some of these pearls of wisdom that are so philosophical.

"Be compassionate, give generously, and subdue your senses. And you will experience great happiness."

"Knowledge of the *Atman* based on one's experience, is gained by meditating on it single-mindedly, and such meditation itself is the act of propitiating it. It alone brings self-satisfaction."

"Becoming first free from all desires, the Almighty dwelling in all creatures should then be brought to the mind. The meditation will then be satisfactory and the objective of life will be achieved."

"The innermost Self is God Himself, and He who is God is also the Guru. There is not the slightest difference amongst these three."

"To experience the oneness of the Self in all beings is the utmost limit of all Knowledge. Emancipation and Bliss are really born from such knowledge."

"Sweetness may depart and from the eye its sparkle, but never will my simple, faithful devotee be without me."

"Prosperity is never permanent, and as for this body, it is forever transient. Knowing that death is always near, conduct yourself according to *dharma.*"

"Wealth is beneficial to the wealthy in so far as it is spent on *dharma* and in charity. For, ethical conduct and charity alone make for true knowledge."

"Whatever pleasure one finds in the five sense-objects, ultimately turns into pain. Truly, nothing is so painful as ignorance!"

"When ignorance is removed and sensual pleasures are given up, the agitated mind will be emancipated from the thraldom of *maya,* and the creature will turn towards Self-realisation, which will bring him the highest bliss."

"This creation is full of numerous forms with varied names. All these are different forms of *maya.* Similarly, the desire of the Spirit, which goes beyond the *Trigunas* — *Sattva, Rajas and Tamas* — that is the manifestation of the Dweller in the heart. Apart from the name and the form, the `You' that remains behind, that is the mark of God. Know this and surrender to Him."

"With a steadfast faith in his mind, he who is engaged in guru-worship, to him God is altogether indebted, and none can cast an evil eye upon him."

"Worldly desires are of various types. But once the significance of 'Who I am' is understood, they melt away as the hailstones by the heat of the sun's rays."

"Only when there is a realisation that the intellect, mind and other sense organs are but gross instruments of the physical body, true detachment will appear, unveiling real knowledge."

"Oblivion of the self is itself the appearance of *maya.* Realisation of the Pure Bliss within is the Essence of all being."

"To experience the bliss of consciousness is to be in that pure state which is knowledge."

"This *Atman* is Brahman; pure consciousness and bliss are Brahman."

Truly, this immeasurable creation of the movable and the immovable is really Baba's very Self!

8

Preachings of Mortality

Maya (illusion) holds us all under her powerful spell so much and for so long. We hardly ever think that temporary pleasures fail to satisfy us, and that as one desire is fulfilled another follows and often these pleasures contain the seeds of pain. Our desire being so inordinate, we do not hesitate to commit bad *karma* in pursuing our pleasure. Whatever atonement we may have made by our sufferings is offset by the craving that we develop for these pleasures. Temporal pleasures are in these ways transient, and become breeding grounds for bad tendencies and bad *karma*. In other words, nothing is Reality, everything is *maya*. The only thing real is Truth.

The illusion or *maya* that surrounds us in nature, called the phenomenal universe and the three *gunas* — *satva*, *rajas* and *tamas* — impel us to act. We are compelled to be reborn to undergo the results of our actions, good or bad. And in every birth we commit more *karmas* which entangle us in more rebirths from which there seems to be no way to come out. Our good *karmas* lead us to a guide or guru. And fortunate indeed are those who found in Sai Baba their guru!

This world is created out of *maya*. They are both thus related to each other as cause and effect. In this manifest world it is *maya* who has assumed a form. Prior to the creation of the world, *maya* had not manifested herself but was absorbed in the Supreme and gathered together in the Unmanifest. Manifest or Unmanifest, *maya* has always been a part of the Supreme Being. Hence this *maya* is the Supreme Being and quite inseparable from It.

Maya created material objects, lifeless and motionless, from *Tamoguna* or Inertia. With this first act of creation, she then, as *Rajoguna* (Motion), combined with the Life force of the Supreme Being, opened up a whole world of consciousness, a variety of moving creatures, by virtue of the aspects of both. The *Sattvaguna* or Righteousness of this *maya* then created the intellect, which, when permeated with the Divine Bliss, completed the process of creation. Thus if *maya*, susceptible to numerous modifications, is not stirred into action, the *Trigunas* remain unmanifest, and so does she.

All the visible world is Brahman, that is, the Supreme Being, *maya* and the world are one. One who can discriminate between the real and the unreal can hope to experience the highest Bliss.

Baba's theory of *maya* was significant. He would say, "Even though I am a *fakir,* freeing myself from all care, without the encumbrances of a house and a family, and am sitting in one place, calm and serene, abandoning all cares and vexations of life, still this irrestrainable *Maya* harasses me, time and again. I am well to forget her, but she never forgets me, but clings fast to me, all the time! She is the *Adimaya* of Shri Hari, who had distracted even Brahma and other gods! But when Hari is pleased, only then will she be destroyed. There is no release from *Maya* unless you ceaselessly sing sai *bhajans."*

When one begins to consider the worldly life as transient, the illusory creation around us faces one, and the traveller is utterly confused, not knowing which way to proceed. This universe is such an illusion, the *maya* or deceptive sport of the Almighty or the Infinite Consciousness.

Maya is an optical illusion. Waves rise and dash against the shore during a stormy weather, and these waves break up into innumerable bubbles that appear as froth. All these bubbles, froths, waves, eddies are different forms of the same water, and are all optical illusions. Likewise, *maya* too takes different forms, but in essence is just illusion.

This being, the *jeevatma,* is beyond the *trigunas*, but being ensnared by *maya*, forgets his divine nature of Truth, Consciousness and Bliss, and he identifies himself with the body. Then he begins to believe that he is the doer, he is the enjoyer. When calamities set in, he is bewildered and does not know how to wriggle out of them. Such is the power of *maya.* The easiest of all ways then is to remember Sai in your heart. This is the only refuge and the only way to destroy *maya.*

It is *maya* that creates an illusory scene containing this whole creation with its animate and inanimate things. This creation of living and non-living things is only a creation in a mind to which it appears as existing in reality, and is not in fact a manifestation. It is like the desires that come true while asleep, but get shattered on waking up.

When one wakes up, the dreams melt away, and it is only by the Sadguru's explanation of the four great *Mahavakyas* that the Supreme Truth is revealed. These great *Mahavakyas* or aphorisms are: (1) Brahman is Pure Consciousness, (2) You are that Brahman (3) To experience the state that I am not the body or the mind, but the *Sakshi* which is Brahman. And (4) *Atman* who is the *Sakshi* or witness of your mind is Brahman. This revelation from the Sadguru comes only when he is pleased. This is the real Self, self-illumined and infinite, while this created elemental universe is the sport or *maya* of that Creator. As such *maya* has no place in the true Self. This *maya* will be dispelled only with the philosophical knowledge, which is received when the guru awakens the disciple with his instruction.

A total identification with the material is an exercise in futility. This is all transitory, illusory *maya.* To avoid getting entangled in the tentacles of this *maya*, one should surrender with a single-minded devotion to

Baba. Only one who sees God in all the created things, animate and inanimate, can overcome *maya* with certainty.

The whole world is a spectacle of *maya*, who is the cause of the birth of this body, and the working of the body depends on Destiny. The visible universe is the unmanifest *maya* or *avidya*, which is without a beginning.

Ignorance of the true Self is the source of *maya*. Once this *maya* is dispelled by the guru's grace, the knowledge of the true Self emerges. The only means of release for one is God-devotion and worship. A devotee of God has no 'Fall', nor is he bonded to the worldly life. Saints appear in this world, assuming a body through the power of *maya*. When their mission is complete, they merge at once into the unmanifest.

Although God resides in the hearts of all creatures, nobody is aware of this, their own state. Such is the unimaginable and great power of illusion of this *maya*. Knowledge is Self-realisation, and is the basis for dispelling ignorance. But unless devotion to God comes, the power of *maya* cannot be overcome. Just as moss covers clear water, or a mist covers a clear sky, so does this *maya* cover knowledge which is itself self-illuminated.

When a person turns a lighted sparkler or firebrand round and round quickly, an illusory ring of fire is produced, this being the inconceivable doings of *maya*. In actuality, it is only fire, and there is no place for a ring of fire. Similarly is this creation which is only an illusion. It is only by dispelling this illusion that *Jnana* or knowledge manifests.

Maya is a marketplace of variegated things that are real and fake. Many purchase the fake. mistaking them for the real. When the Sadguru shows why a fake looks like the real, ignorance disappears, and only Knowledge remains. Know that what remains is the Truth.

Maya being illusory, identification of the body with the real Self and attachment to it is called 'death' by the wise. It is very difficult indeed to cross this ocean of worldly life with *maya* weaving a web of illusion. Therefore, do not get entangled in her meshes, but surrender to God-worship and devotion. Devotion to one's guru will help one cross this illusory state, and step into Truth.

9

Creator's Creation

Sai Baba would always say, "I shall remain active and vigorous even after leaving this earthly body.... My shrine will bless my devotees and fulfil their needs.... I am ever living to help those who come to me and surrender, and seek refuge in me." Though he left his mortal coils, he is even today 'alive' with his continued presence. You have only to remember him and chant his name, and he is there for you, but be sure to have a pure heart.

There was a rehearsal of Baba's death as early as in 1886. He instructed Mahlsapati thus, "I am going to Allah (*showing the formlessness*). Take care of this body for three days. If I return, I will look after it myself. If not, bury it in that open land and put up two posts to mark the place."

Baba's breathing and circulation stopped. The civil authorities held an inquest, and pronouncing him dead, ordered Mahlsapati to bury or cremate the body. This instruction was in accordance with the law that a dead body was not to be kept longer that twenty four hours in those days. Mahlsapati, of course, refused to comply with the orders, and safeguarded Baba's body as if it belonged to his own self.

On the third day, Mahlsapati's joy knew no bounds when the body resumed breathing, and Sai Baba opened his eyes! His fame, no doubt, spread like wildfire after this incident. Blessed are the people who enjoyed the rare happiness of Baba's company for more than half a century!

From 1910, Baba's health gradually began to weaken and taking upon himself the burden of his devotees.

On Vijayadashami day in 1916, Baba had an attack of frenzy. He tore off his clothes, and standing stark naked for nearly two hours, cried out, "Now decide, decide for yourselves whether I am a Muslim or a Hindu!" He cried out that it was his day of 'crossing the frontiers'. It was on the same day two years later, on October 15, 1918, that he attained *samadhi*.

Before attaining his *samadhi*, he gave instructions to various people, but none seemed to have grasped the point of these dispositions. He gave some money from the pocket of his *kafni* to Laxmibai Shinde who had served him faithfully in the mosque, and lovingly brought him eatables every day at the appointed time without fail. Though she was well-off, yet to her these nine rupees were unique, a treasured gift, for, to her, this was a reminder of Sai to the end of her life.

When Buty had built the *wada*, he wanted to install an idol of Krishna there. Baba told him, "Break the coconut. We, all the children, will pass our time here. All the children will find peace of mind." When Baba breathed his last, it was here that his body was buried, and it was then that the significance of Baba's words struck them. The installation of Krishna's idol had remained unfulfilled till then, but Baba's *samadhi* there proved that it was Sai Baba, who was to occupy that place.

He sent word to a Muslim saint, saying, "The light that Allah lit is fading away," and the saint shed tears of sorrow. He distributed two hundred rupees for feeding *fakirs*, and they sat there reading from the *Quran*.

When his end neared, Baba sent all those who sat around him to eat their lunch. He told Bayaji Kote, "I am going. Carry me to the *wada*", and told him not to reveal what he had said to him. Nana Nimonkar too was beside Baba when Baba breathed his last and lay with his head on Bayaji's lap.

Despite Baba's explicit wish that he should be buried at Buty Wada, there was disagreement about his burial between the Muslims and the Hindus, which was finally amicably settled as per Baba's wishes. It was also agreed that the *wada* and the mosque should be kept open for people of all religions.

By shedding off the physical body, Baba attained to that eternal state which is 'Infinity'. He was manifest in his physical body, but by casting it off he became Unmanifest, merging with his real Self, the 'Infinity'.

When the body and its organs come together, there is birth, and with their separation comes death. To become entangled in the worldly life denotes birth, and being free of it is death. Every birth is followed by death, and every being, on dying, leaves his mortal coils, for death is the natural state of the body. It is life that is the unnatural and pleasurable state of the body.

Whosoever visits Shirdi and Baba's mosque with hope in his heart never returns in despair. Baba used to say, "I am always in the eyes of him who is most fond of me. To him, the whole creation is empty without me, and in his mouth there are tales of me and me alone. He meditates on me ceaselessly, and sings only my praises. And when he becomes one with me, he forgets both action and inaction. Where there is such eagerness and reverence to serve me, only there I wait, all the time." Baba lives on, and only the devoted and faithful can bear testimony to this truth.